THE PHILLIP KEVEREN SERIES
JAZZ STANDARDS

— PIANO LEVEL —
EARLY INTERMEDIATE/INTERMEDIATE
(HLSPL LEVEL 4-5)

ISBN-13: 978-1-4234-0790-4
ISBN-10: 1-4234-0790-3

7777 W. BLUEMOUND RD. P.O. BOX 13819 MILWAUKEE, WI 53213

For all works contained herein:
Unauthorized copying, arranging, adapting, recording or public performance is an infringement of copyright.
Infringers are liable under the law.

Visit Hal Leonard Online at
www.halleonard.com

Visit Phillip at
www.phillipkeveren.com

THE PHILLIP KEVEREN SERIES

PREFACE

We all love a great song. A magical lyric, when paired with a striking melody, has a way of entering the fabric of life and enriching our days. The very best of these songs stand the test of time and become staples in the jazz repertoire. The selections in this collection have become standards because they are superior compositions. They can be arranged in a variety of ways with myriad harmonic settings and still maintain their singular identity.

These are some of my personal favorites. I hope you enjoy playing them at the piano!

Sincerely,
Phillip Keveren

BIOGRAPHY

Phillip Keveren, a multi-talented keyboard artist and composer, has composed original works in a variety of genres from piano solo to symphonic orchestra. Mr. Keveren gives frequent concerts and workshops for teachers and their students in the United States, Canada, Europe, and Asia. Mr. Keveren holds a B.M. in composition from California State University Northridge and a M.M. in composition from the University of Southern California.

THE PHILLIP KEVEREN SERIES

CONTENTS

- 4 ALL OR NOTHING AT ALL
- 9 ALL THE THINGS YOU ARE
- 12 BLAME IT ON MY YOUTH
- 15 BODY AND SOUL
- 18 CHEEK TO CHEEK
- 24 HERE'S THAT RAINY DAY
- 27 I'LL REMEMBER APRIL
- 32 I'VE GOT YOU UNDER MY SKIN
- 37 ISN'T IT ROMANTIC
- 40 LITTLE GIRL BLUE
- 45 LONG AGO (AND FAR AWAY)
- 48 LOVE LETTERS
- 54 LOVE YOU MADLY
- 57 LULLABY OF BIRDLAND
- 60 MY FUNNY VALENTINE
- 63 MY ROMANCE
- 66 SAY IT ISN'T SO
- 69 SKYLARK
- 72 THIS CAN'T BE LOVE
- 75 THE VERY THOUGHT OF YOU

ALL OR NOTHING AT ALL

Words by JACK LAWRENCE
Music by ARTHUR ALTMAN
Arranged by Phillip Keveren

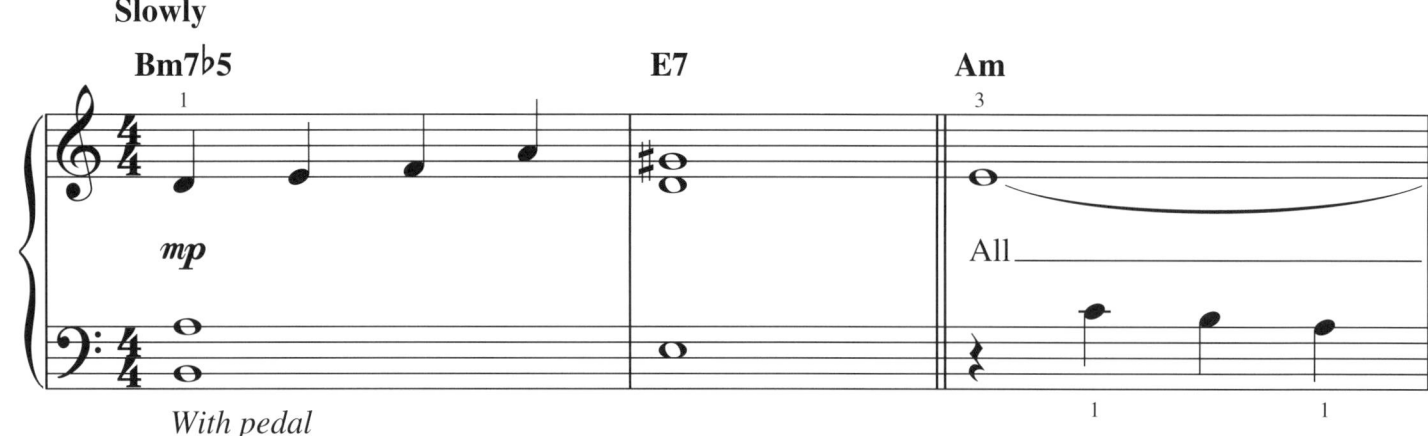

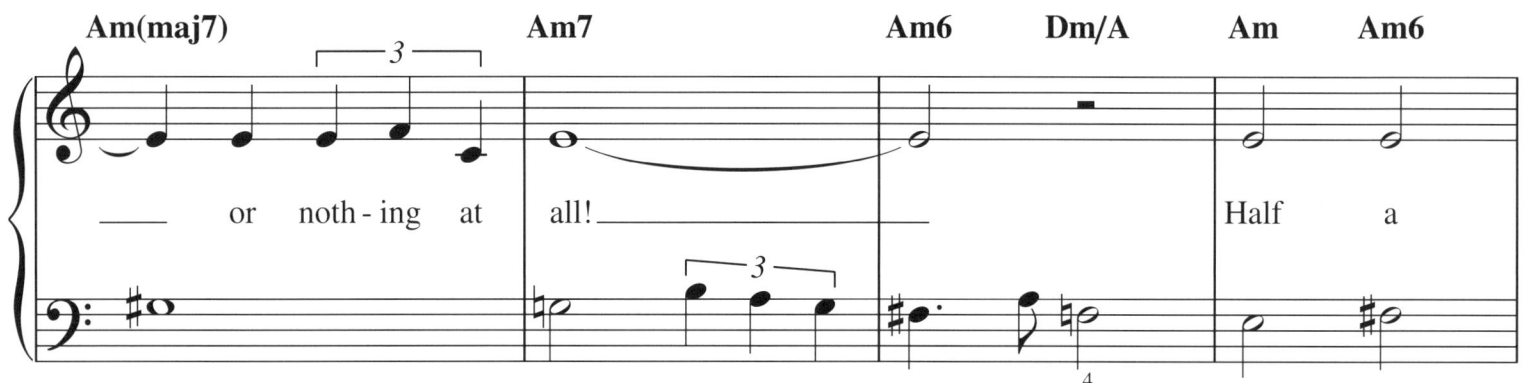

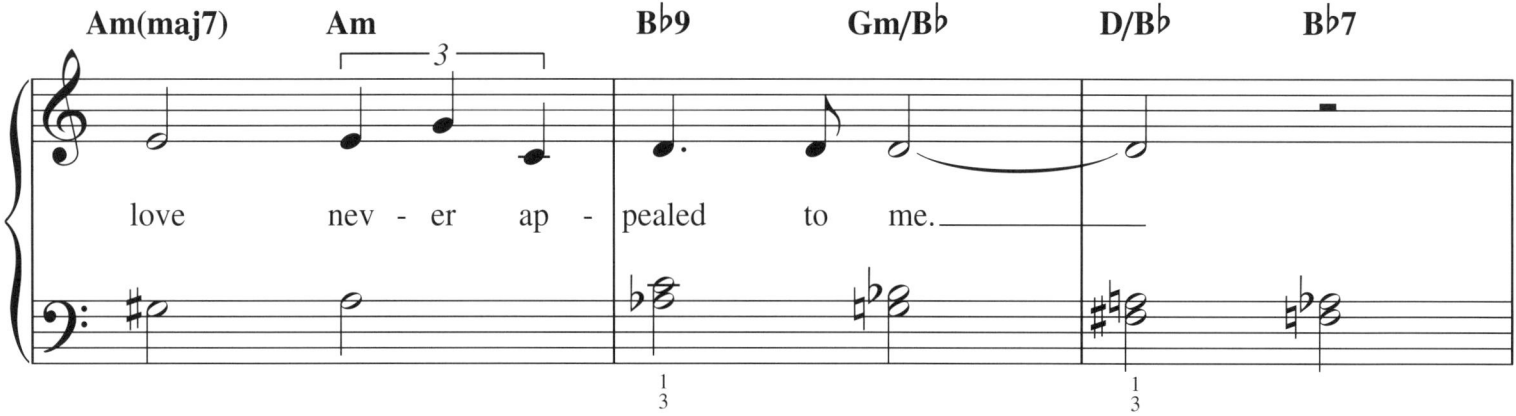

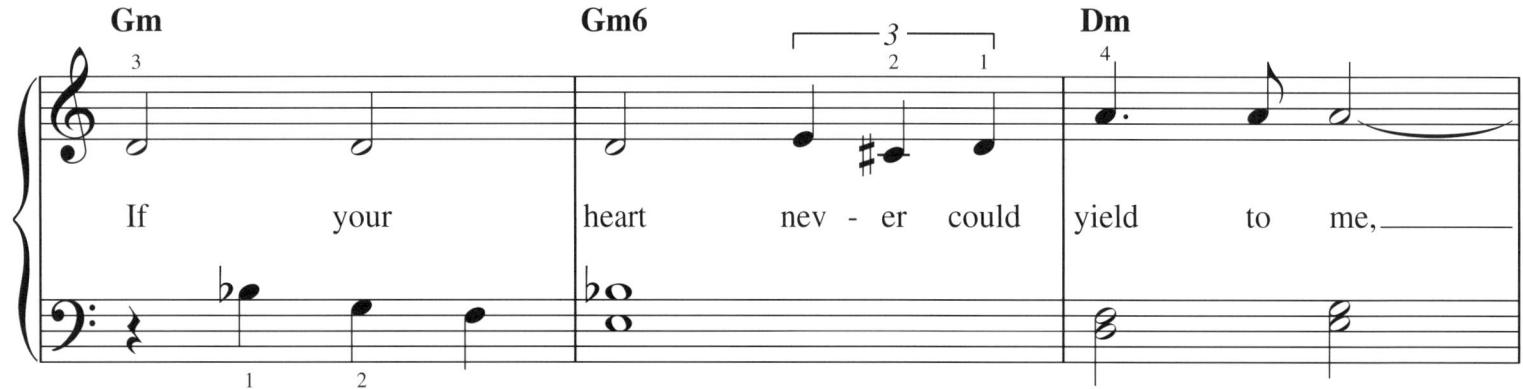

Copyright © 1939 by Universal Music Corp.
Copyright renewed; extended term of Copyright deriving from Jack Lawrence and Arthur Altman assigned and effective June 20, 1995 to Range Road Music Inc.
International Copyright Secured   All Rights Reserved
Used by Permission

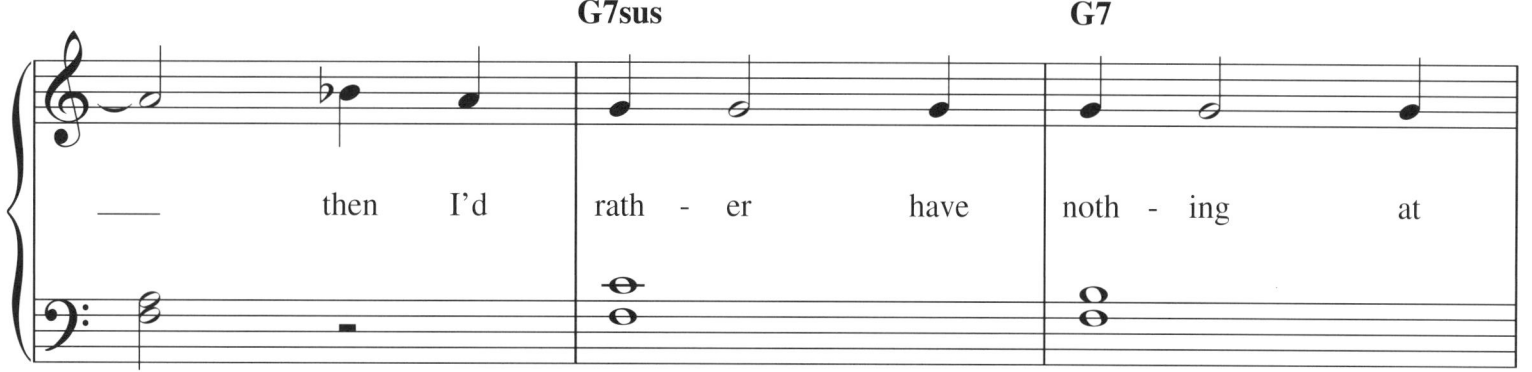
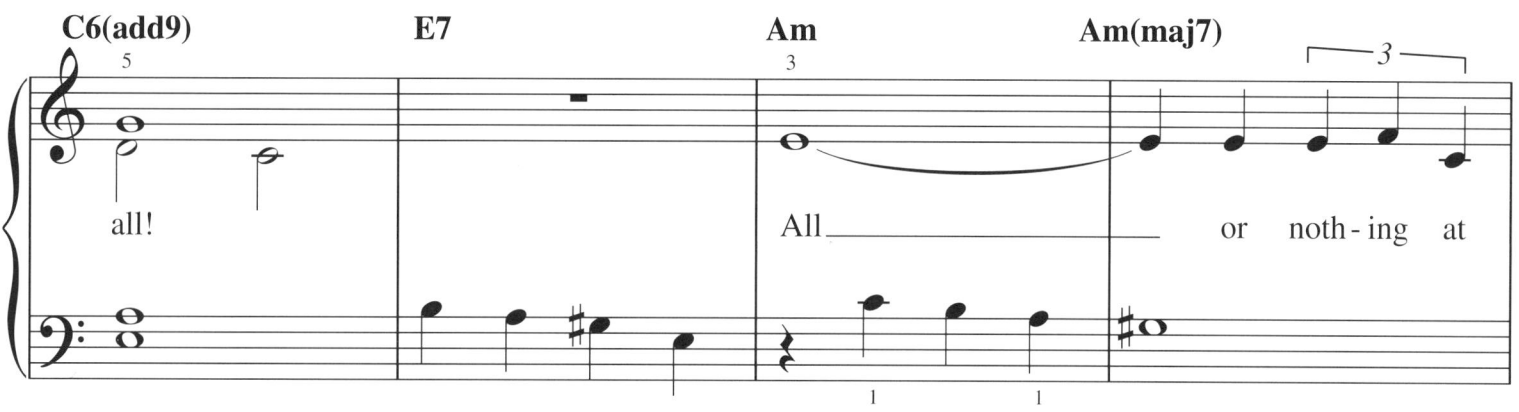
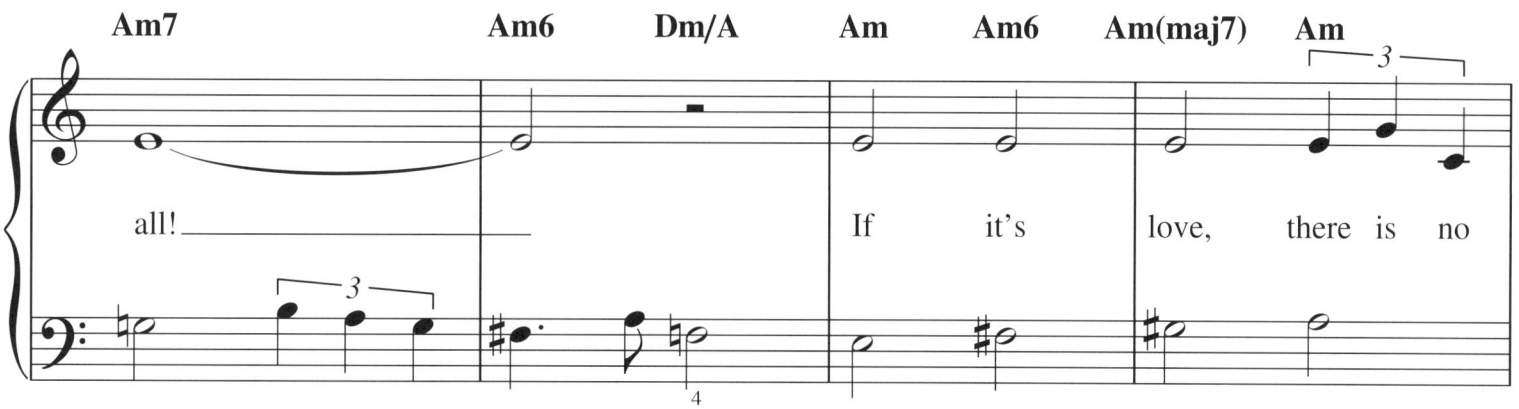
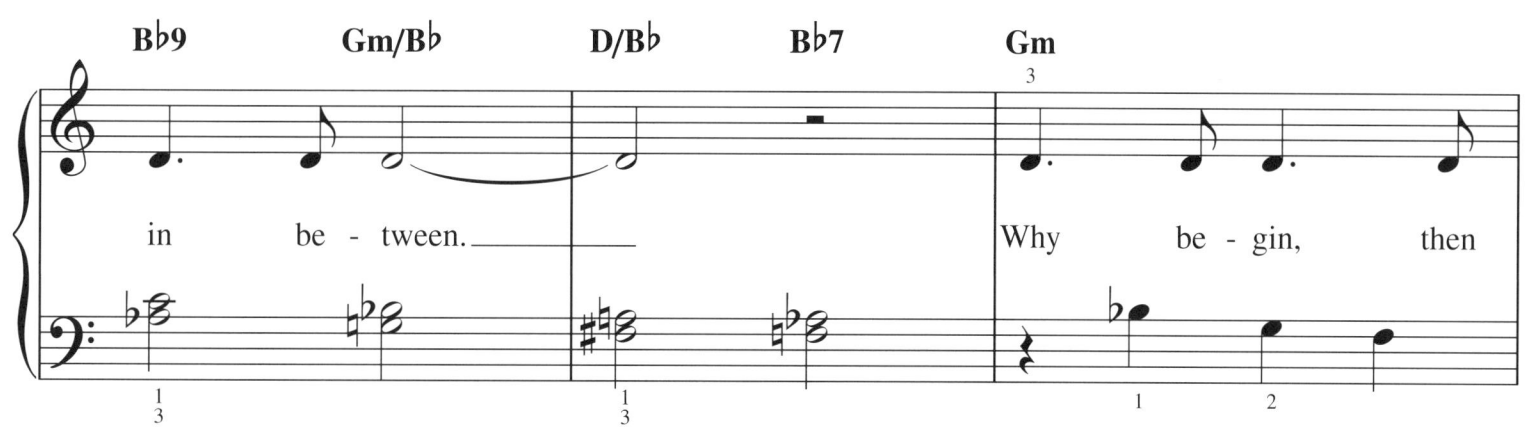

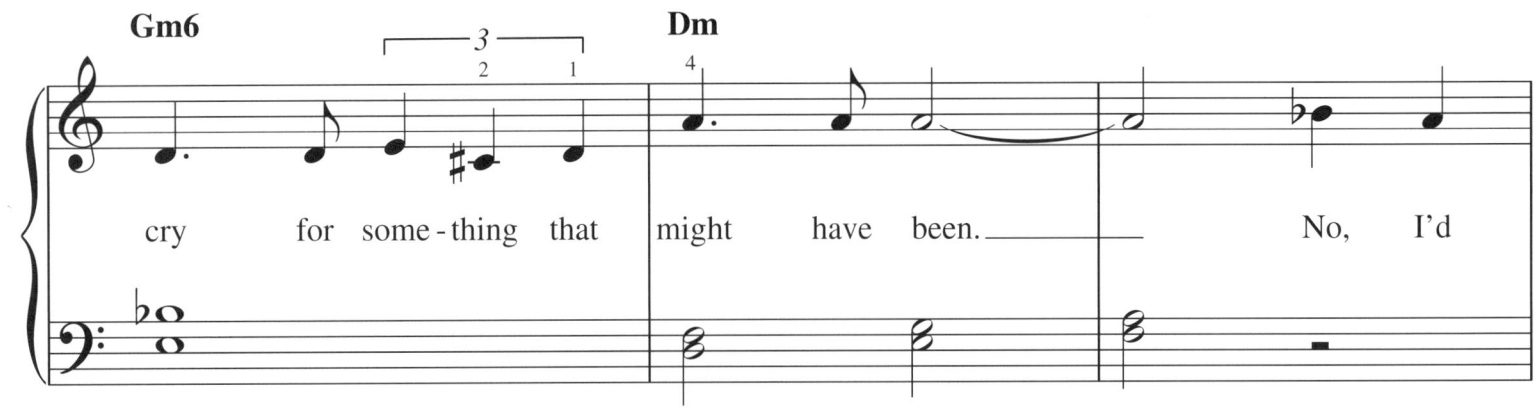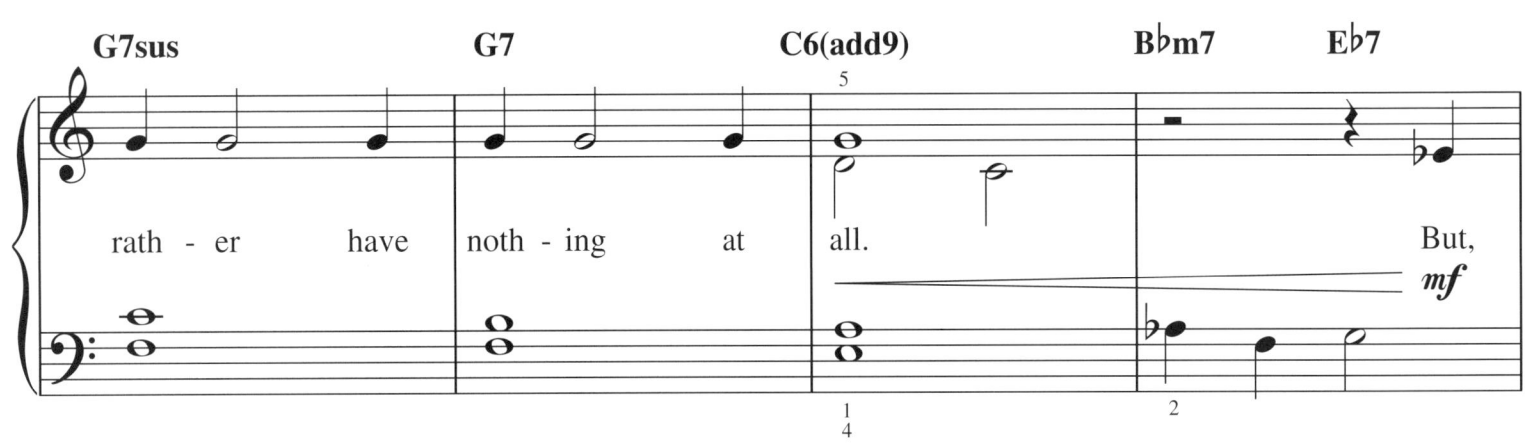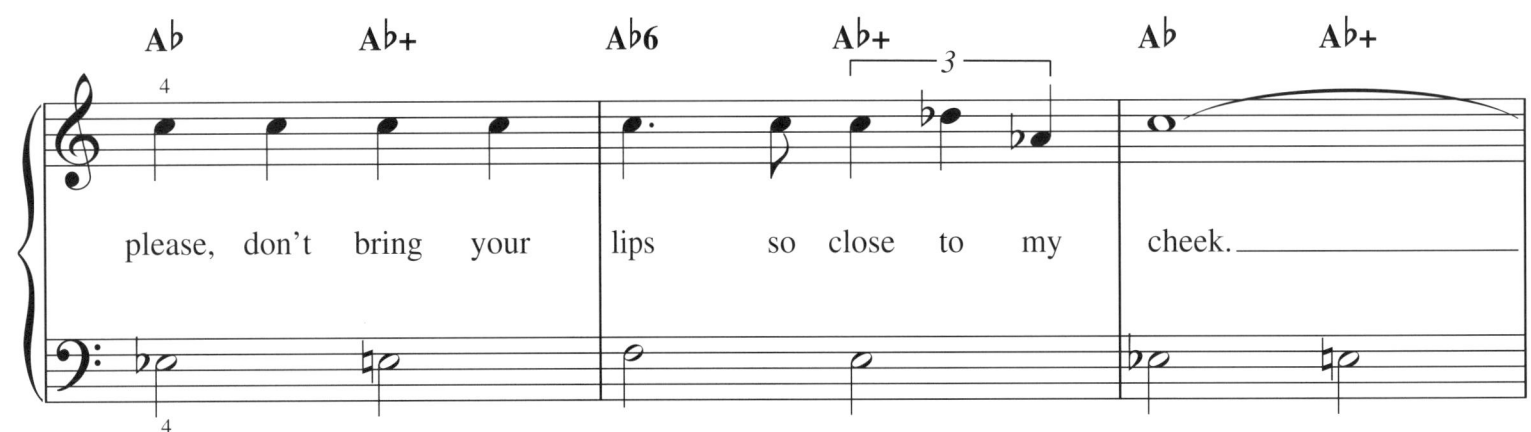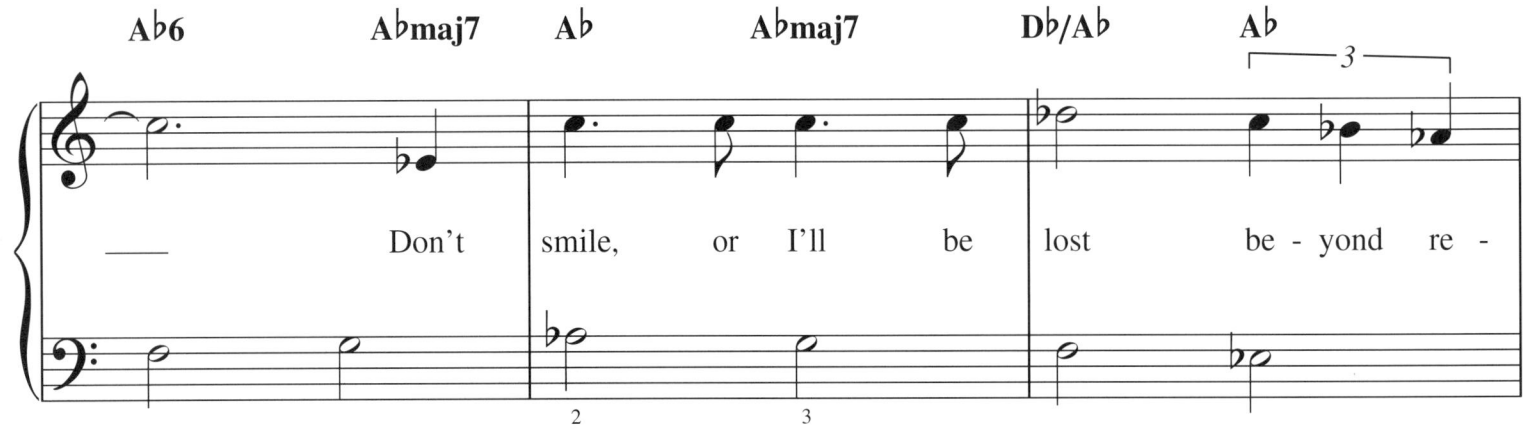

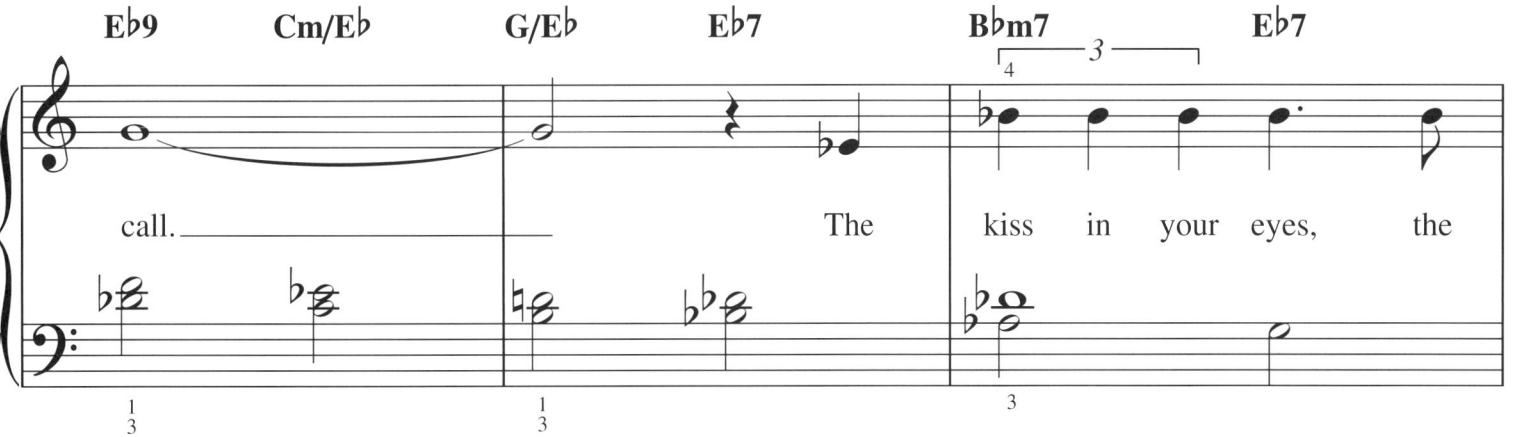
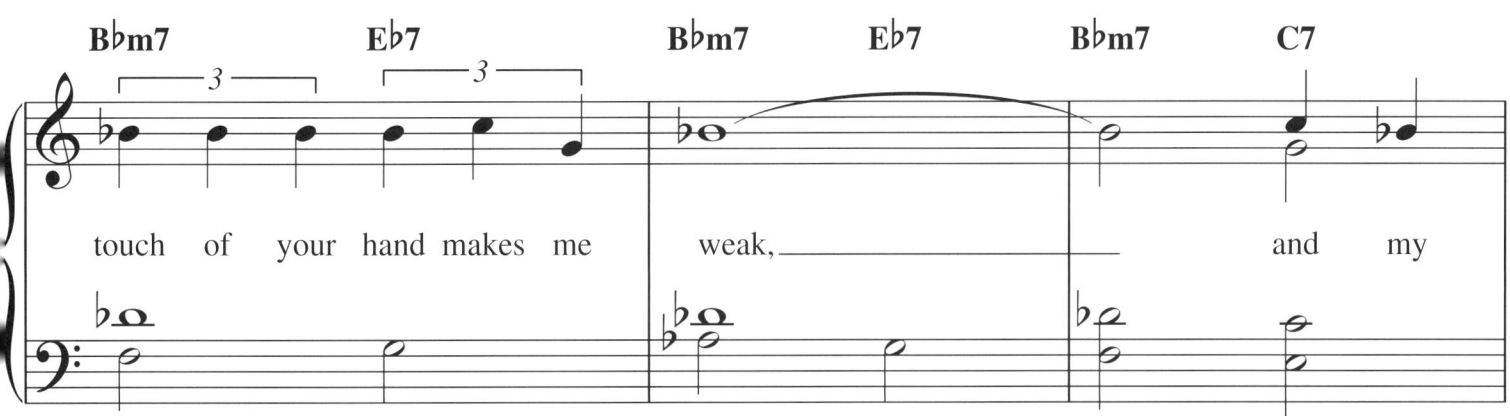
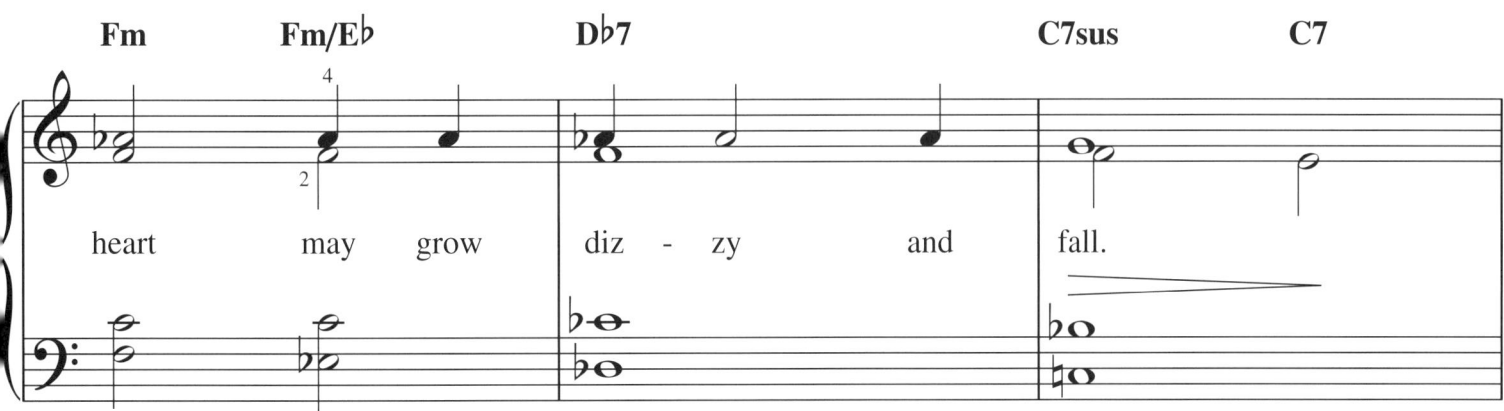
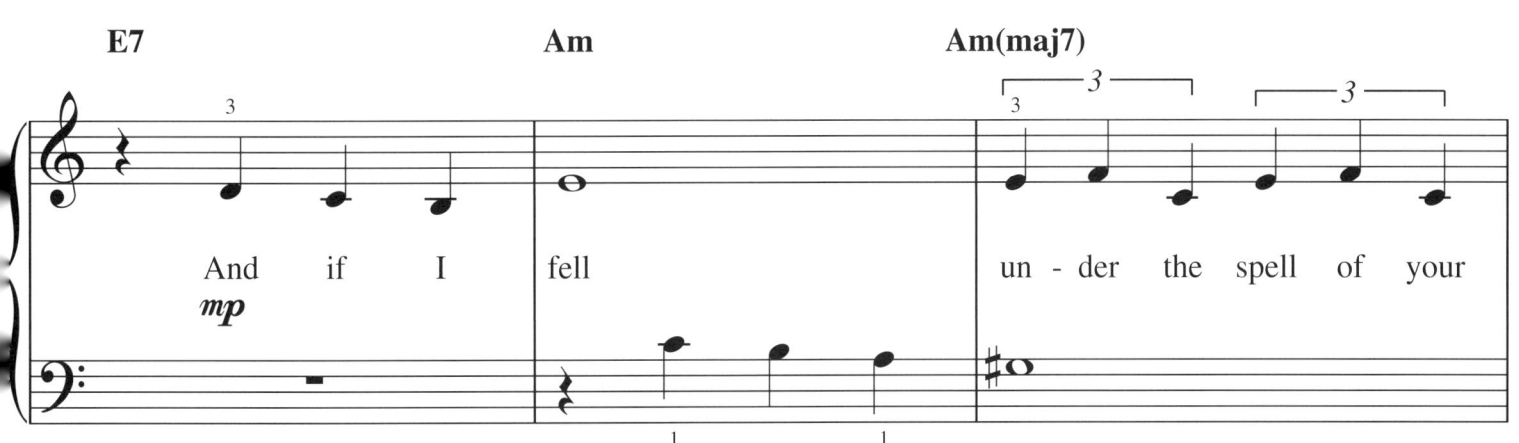

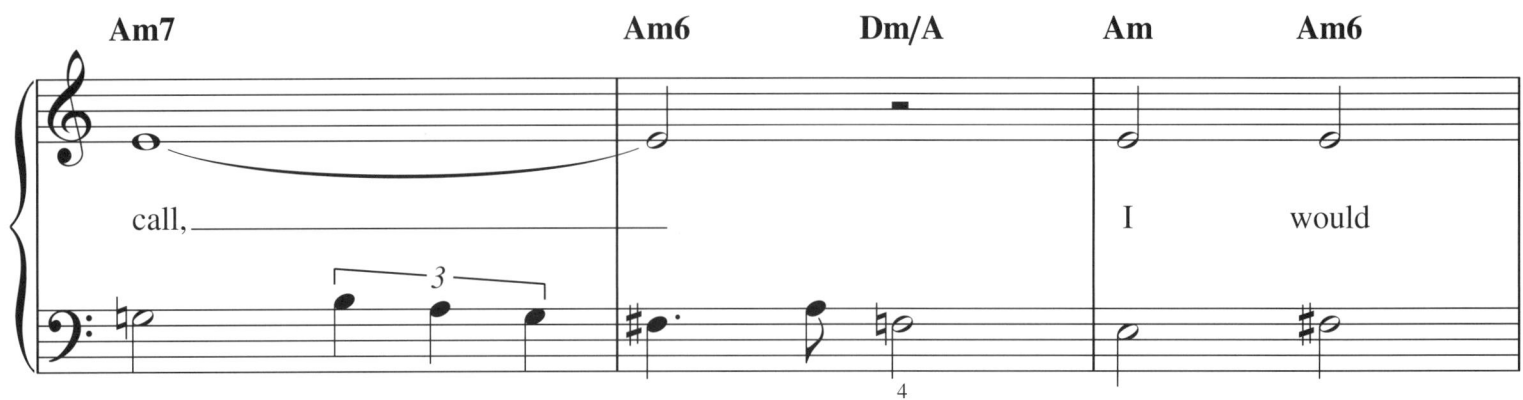
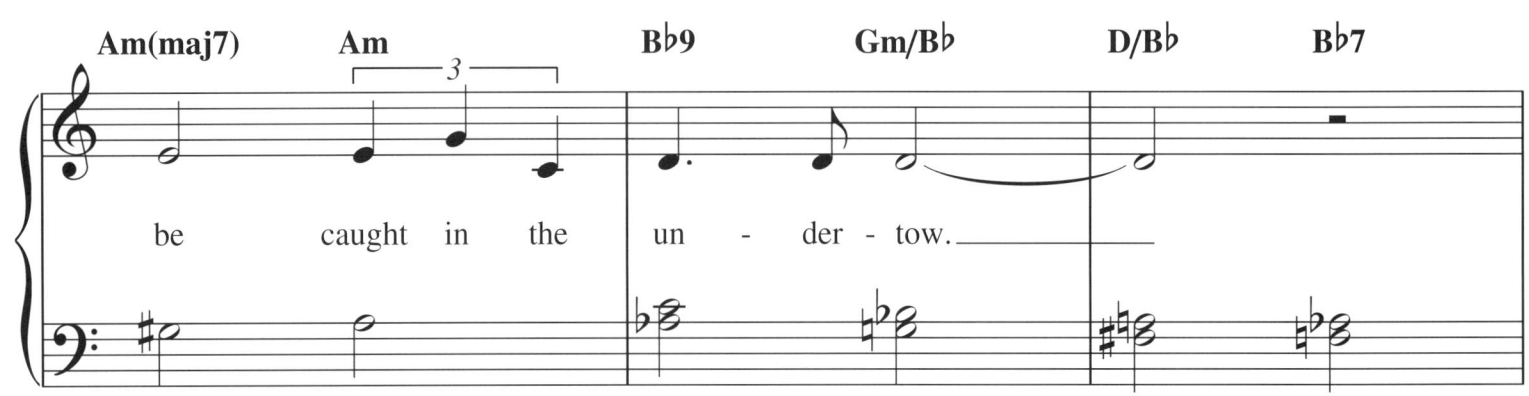

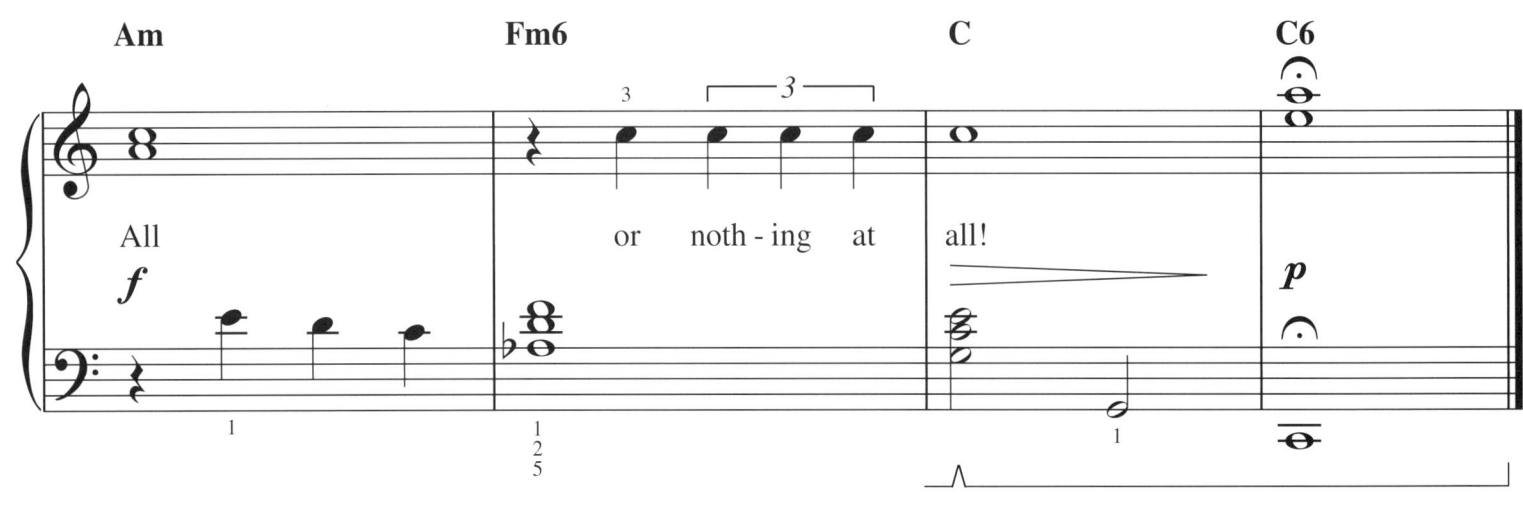

All The Things You Are
from VERY WARM FOR MAY

Lyrics by OSCAR HAMMERSTEIN II
Music by JEROME KERN
Arranged by Phillip Keveren

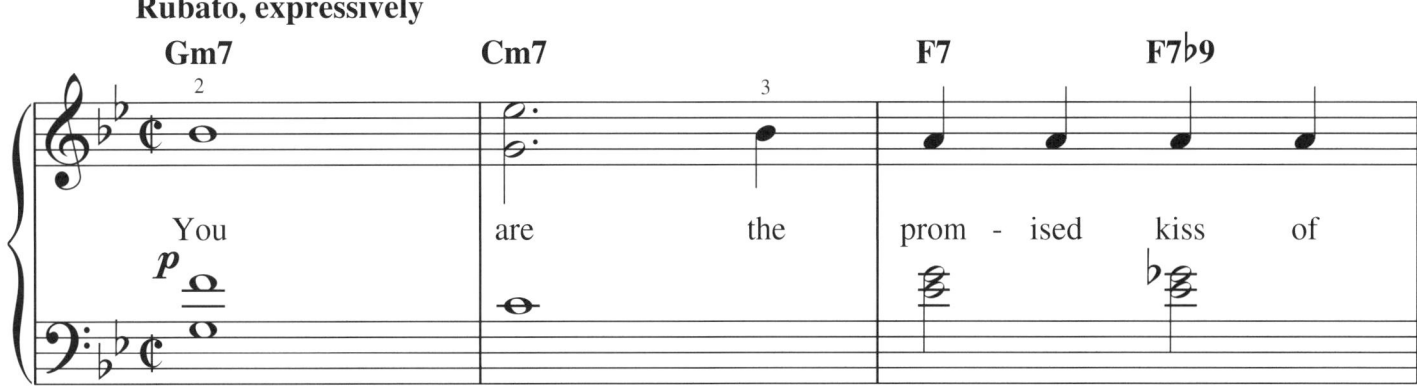

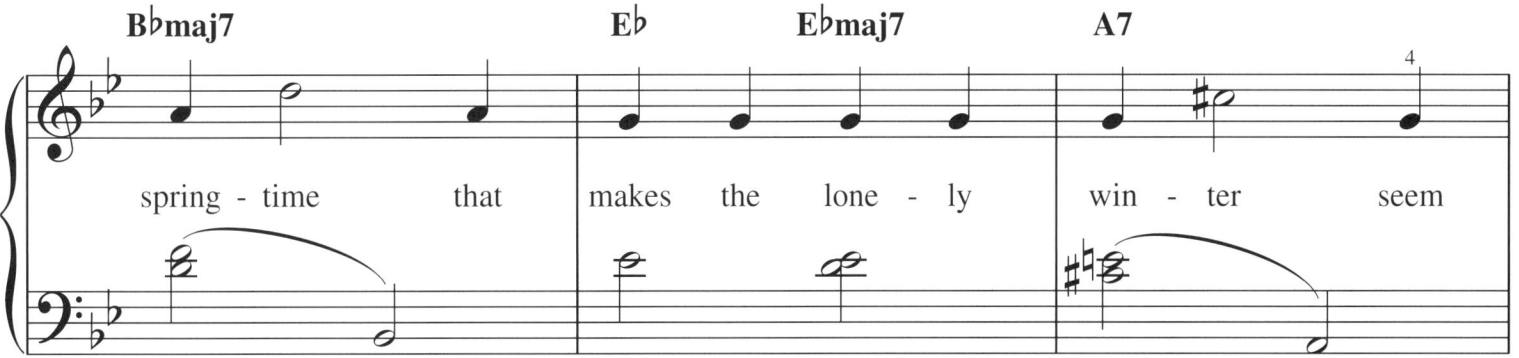

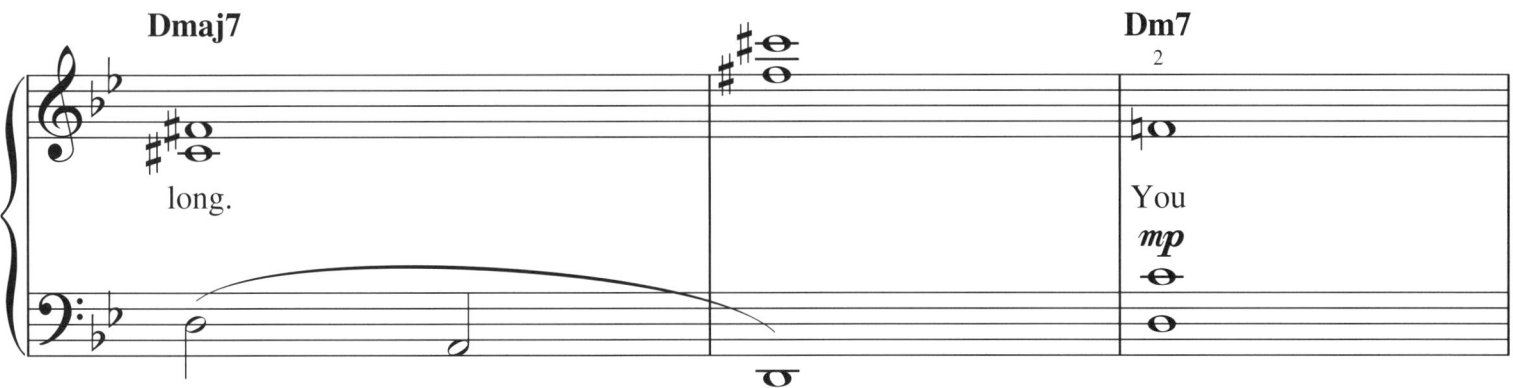

Copyright © 1939 UNIVERSAL - POLYGRAM INTERNATIONAL PUBLISHING, INC.
Copyright Renewed
All Rights Reserved   Used by Permission

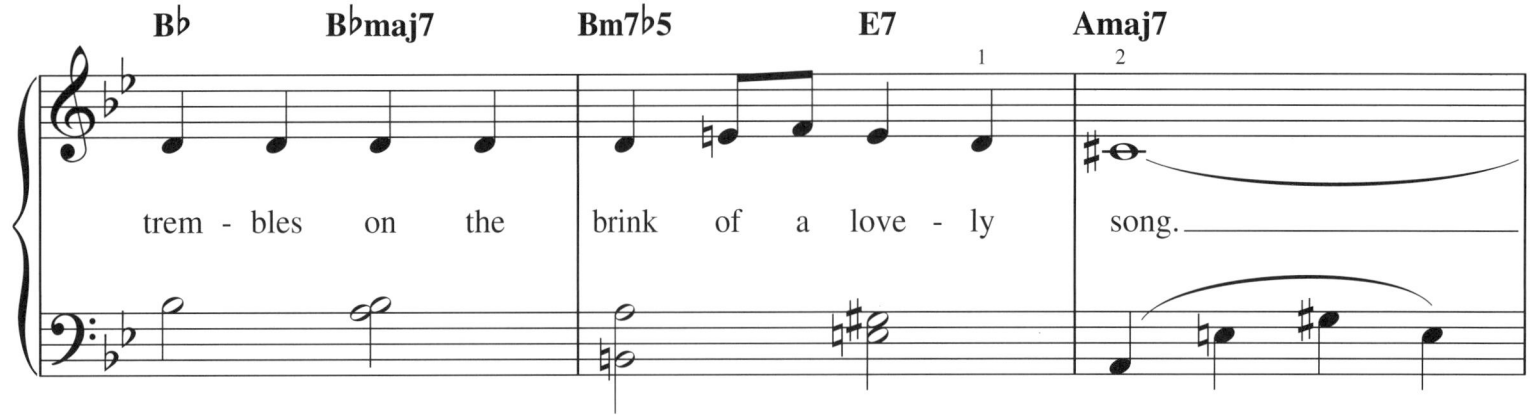
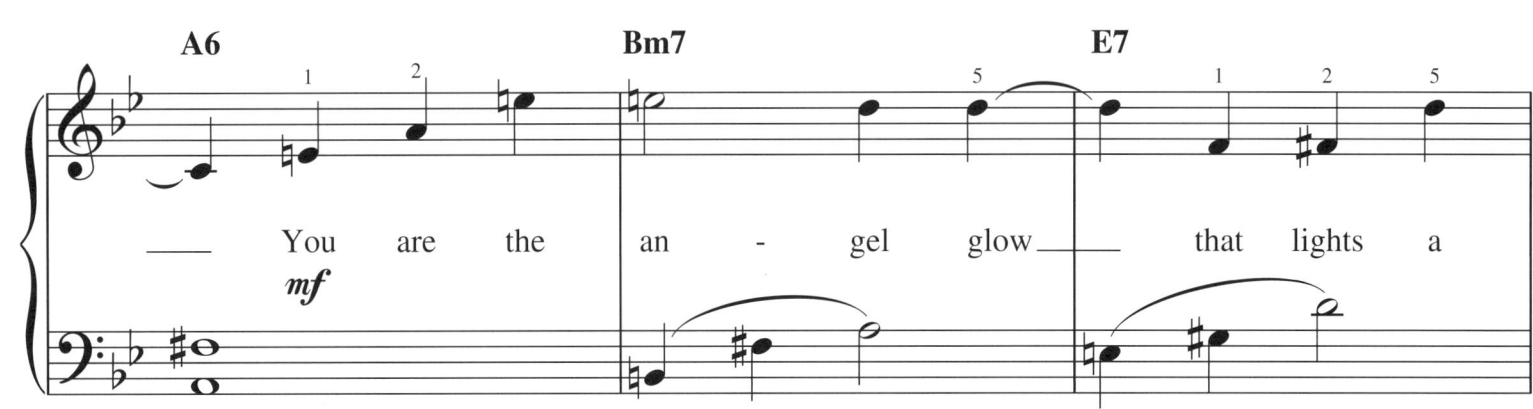
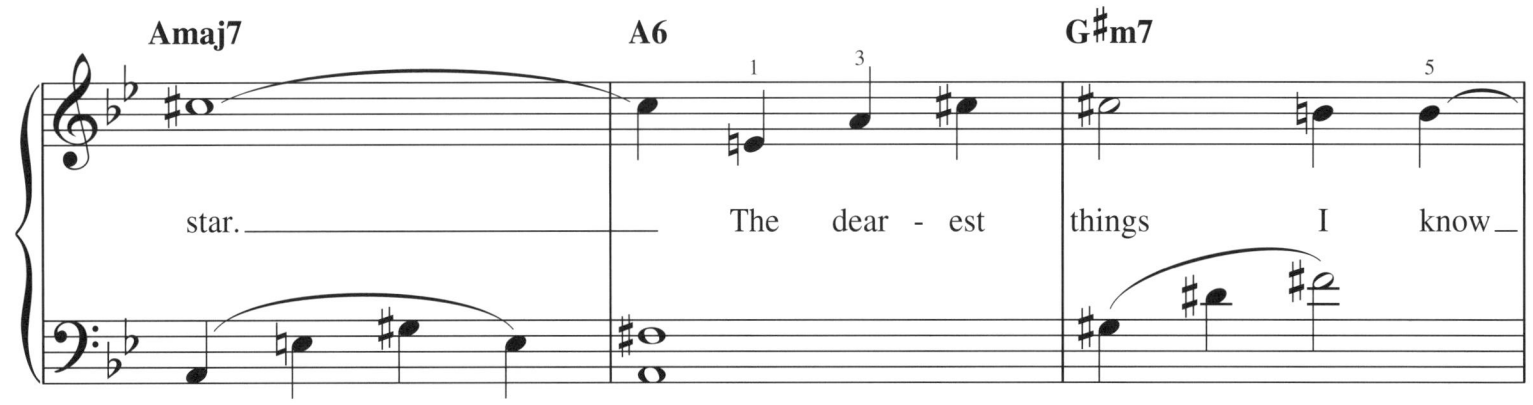
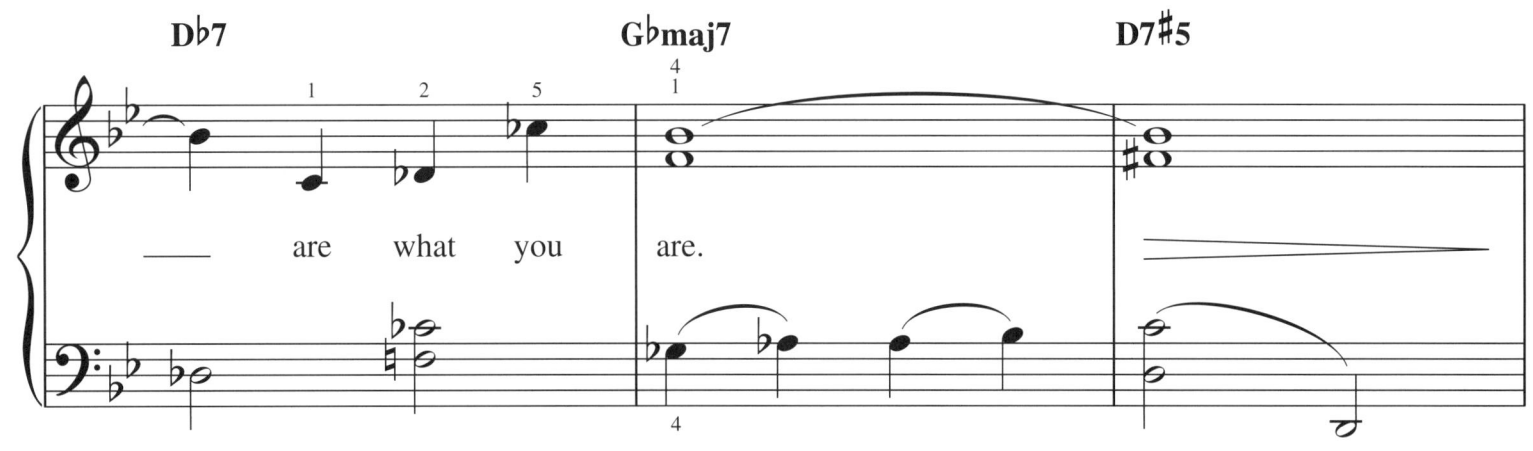

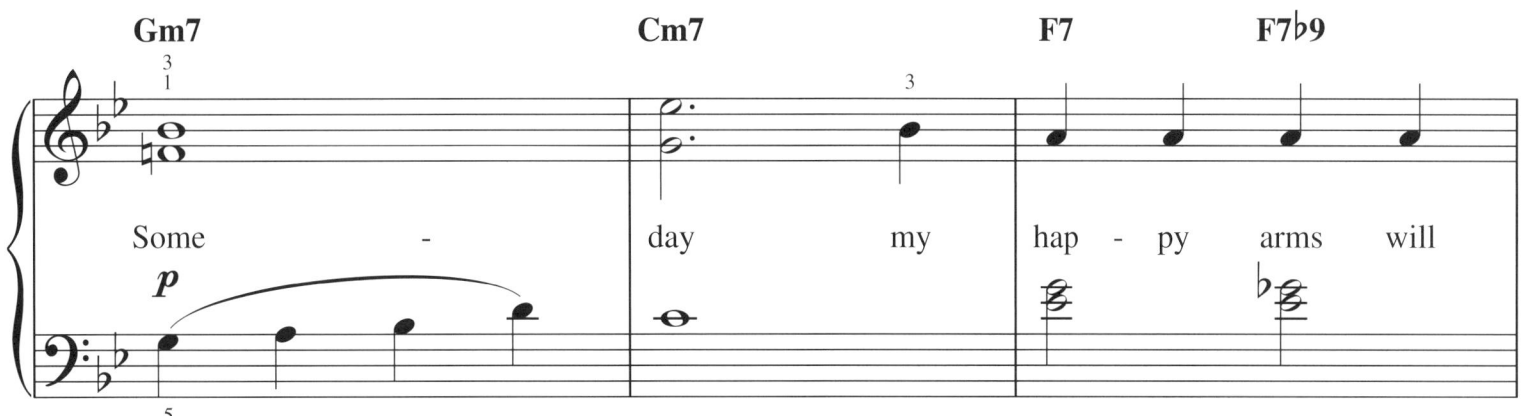
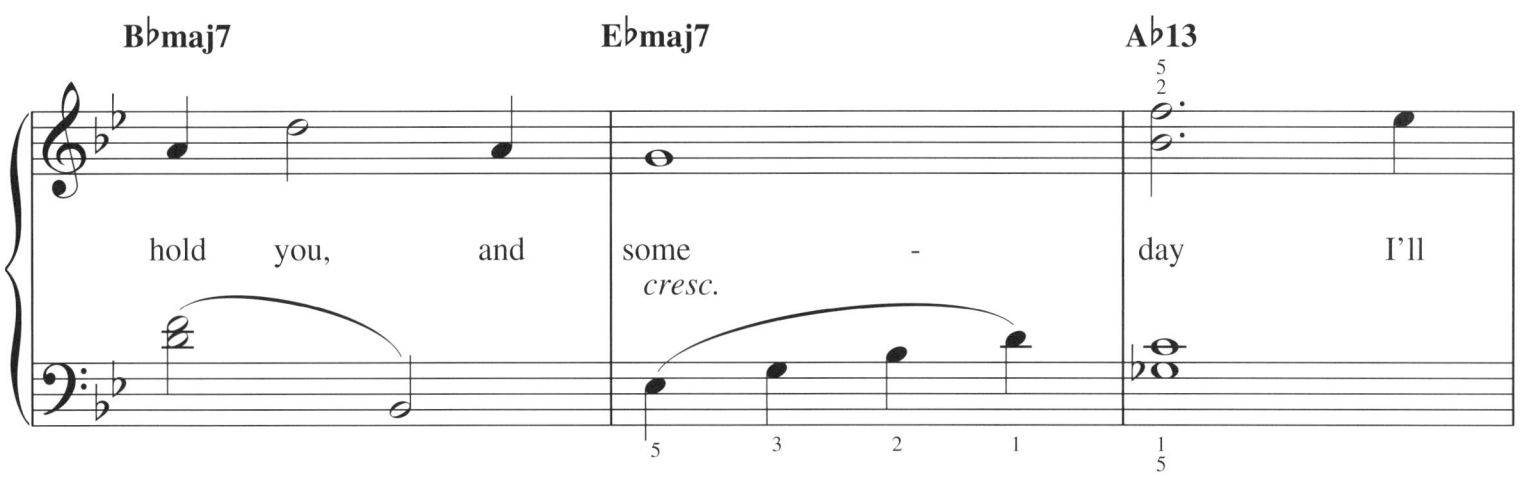
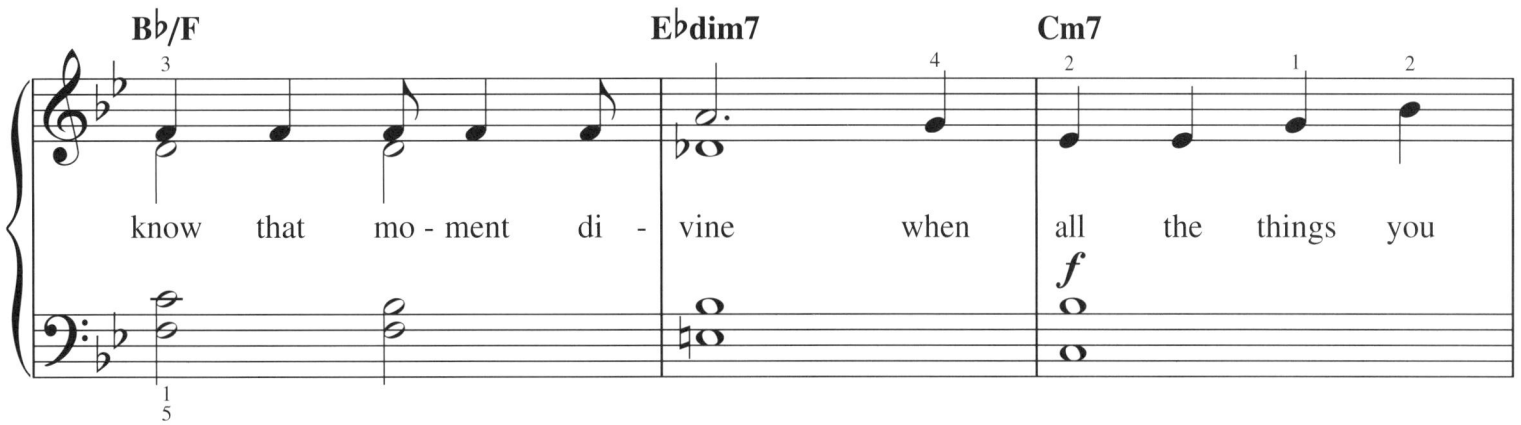
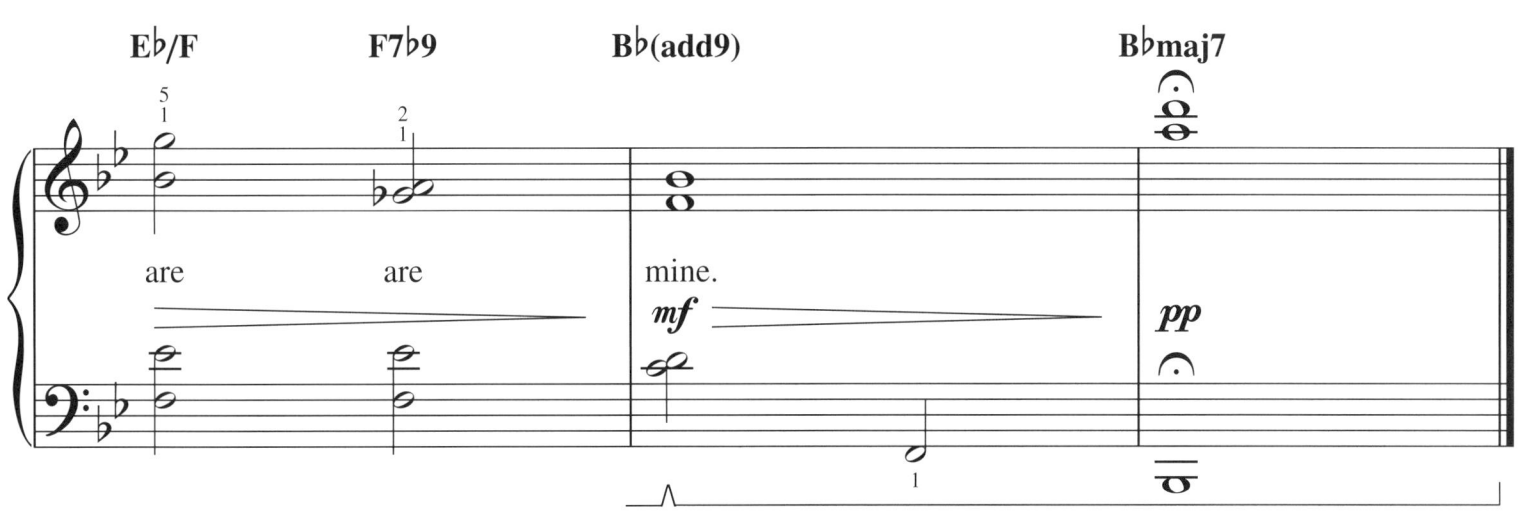

BLAME IT ON MY YOUTH

Words by EDWARD HEYMAN
Music by OSCAR LEVANT
Arranged by Phillip Keveren

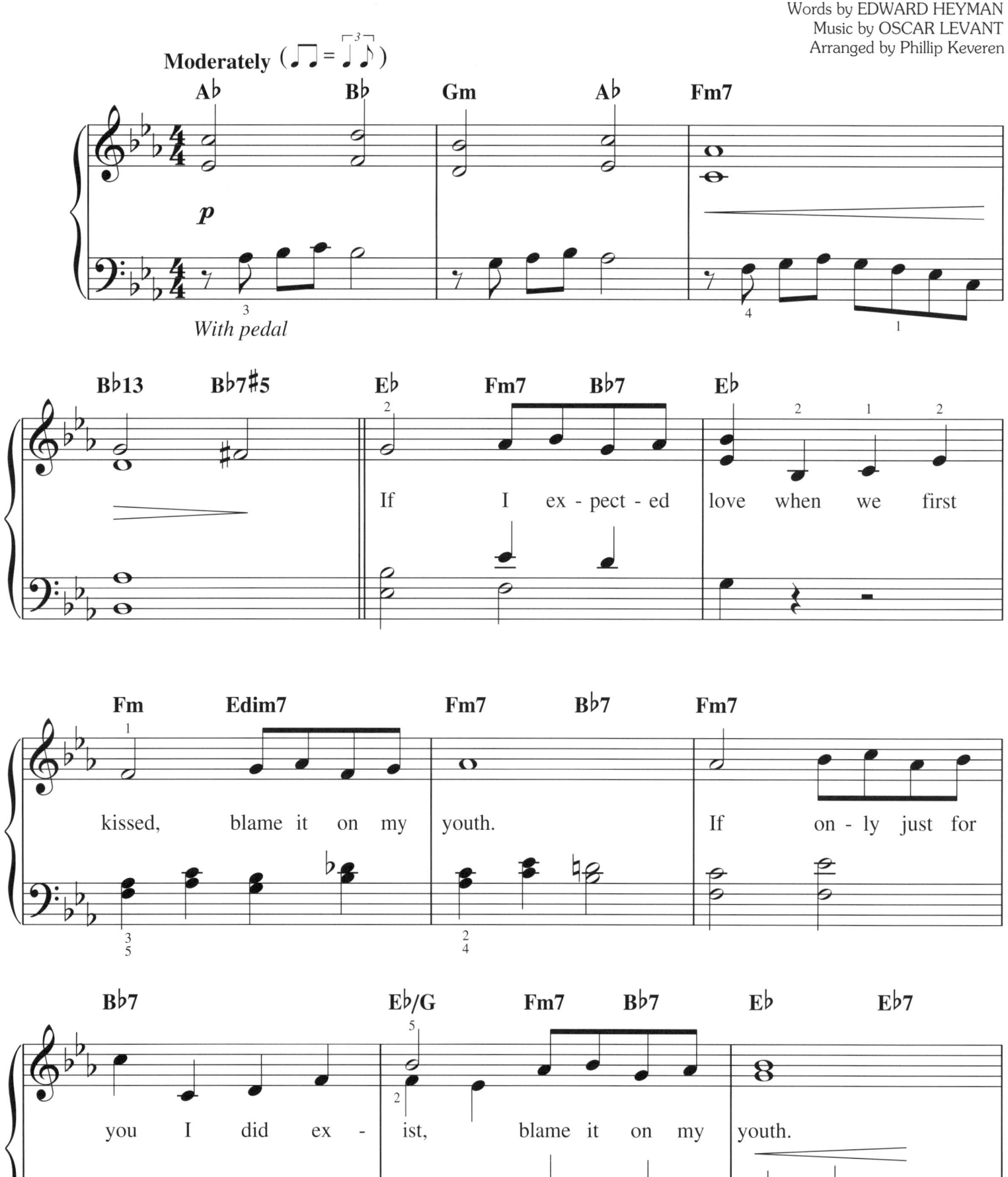

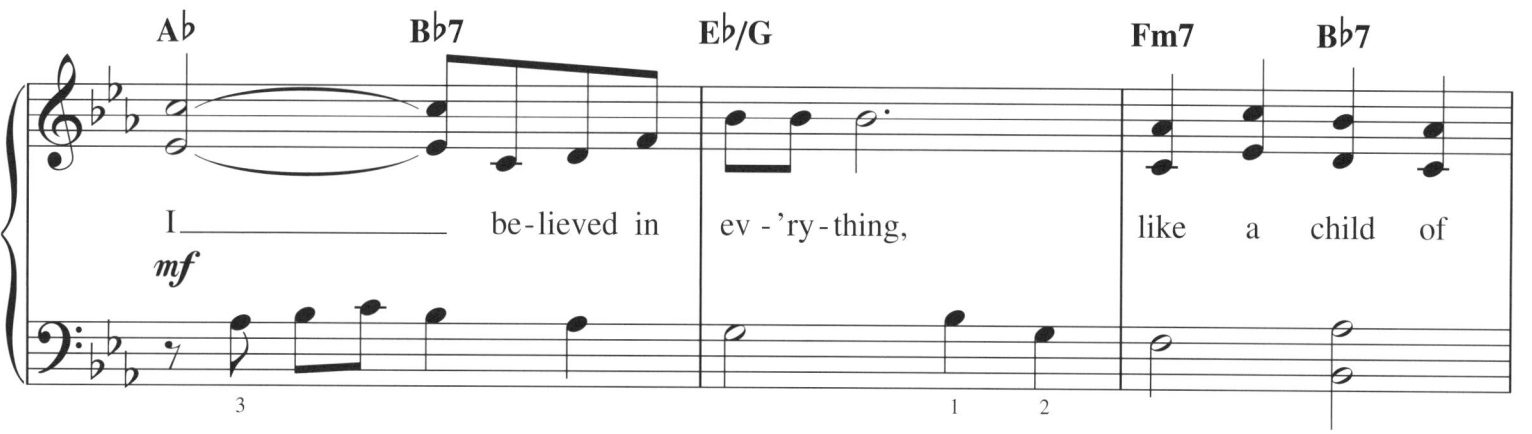
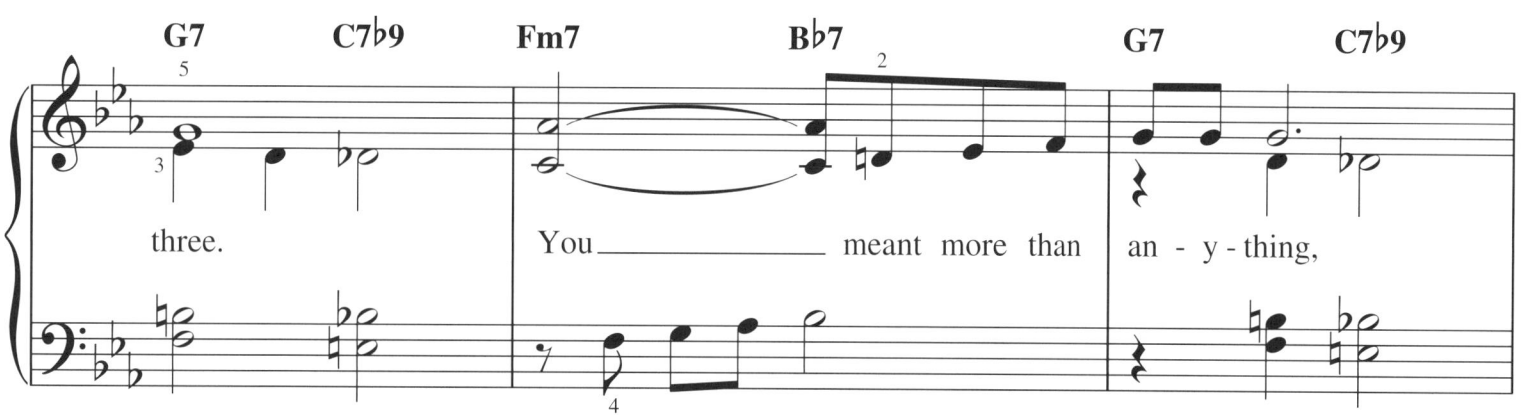
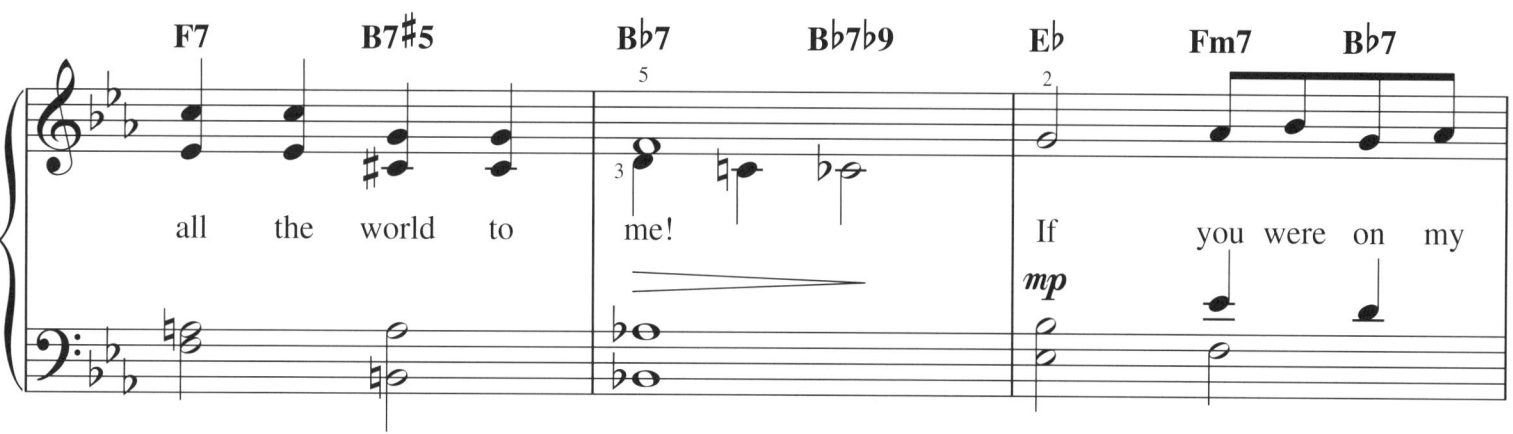

Fm7 B♭7 E♭/G Fm7 B♭7
If I for - got to eat and sleep and pray, blame it on my
E♭ E♭7 A♭ B♭7 E♭/G Edim7
youth. If I cried a lit - tle bit when
mf
Fm7 G7 C7♭9 Fm7
first I learned the truth, don't blame it on my
F7 B♭7 E♭ E♭maj7
heart, blame it on my youth.
rit.
f
p

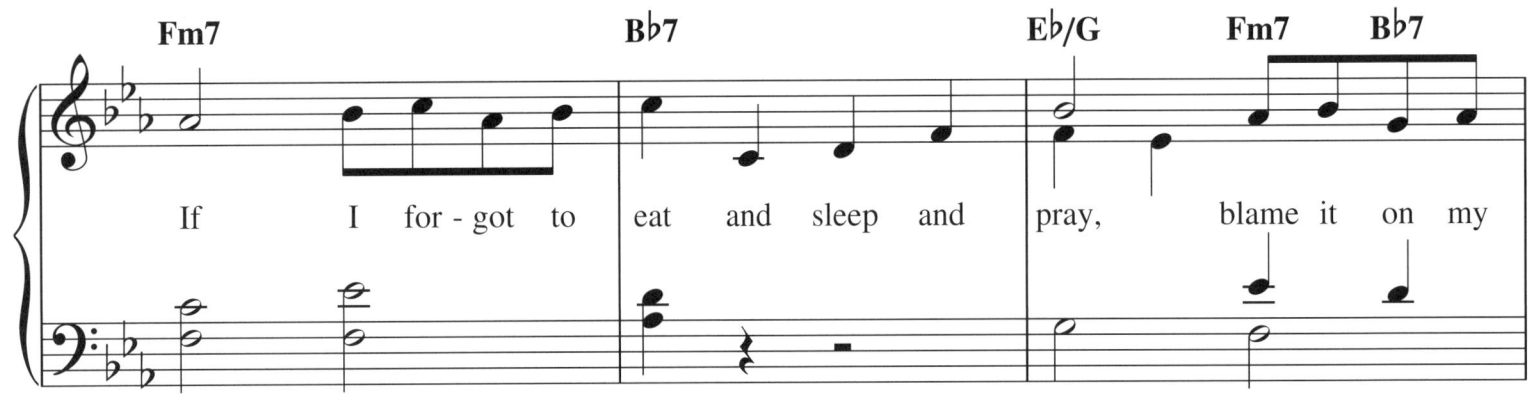

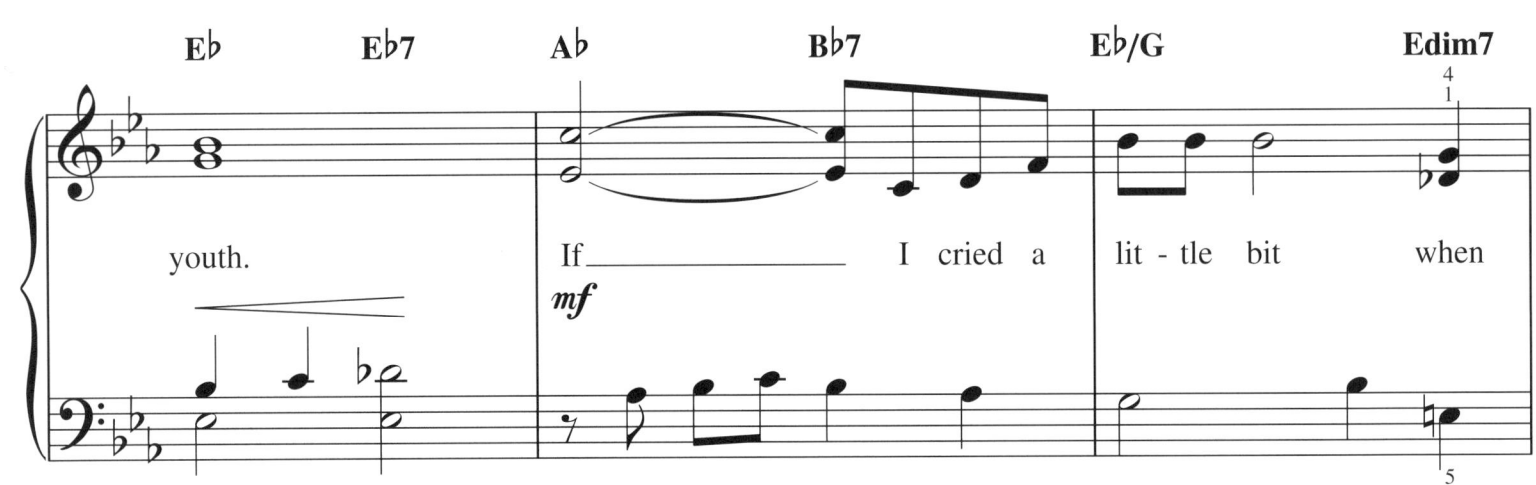

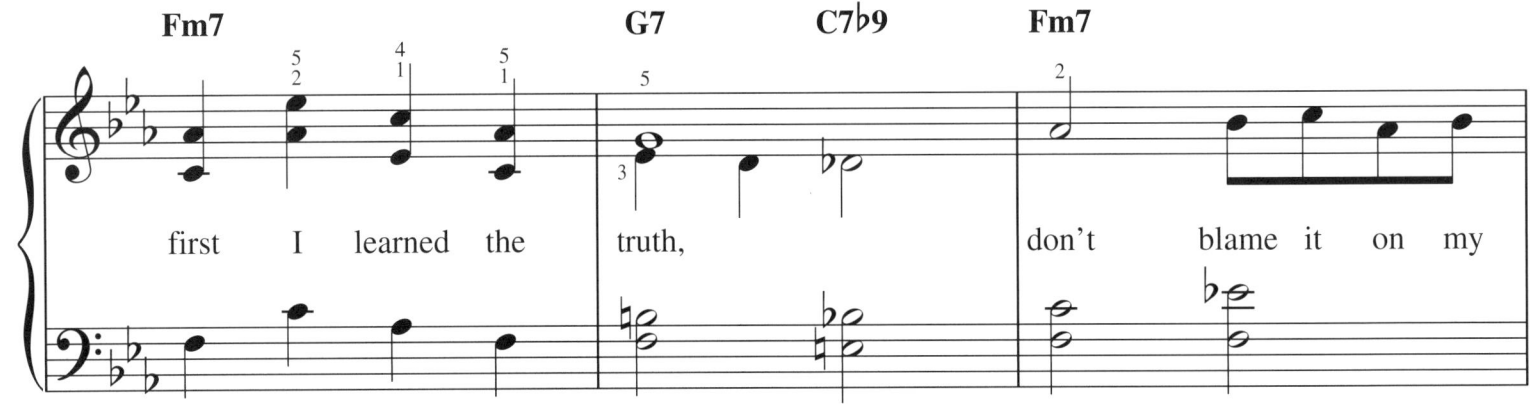

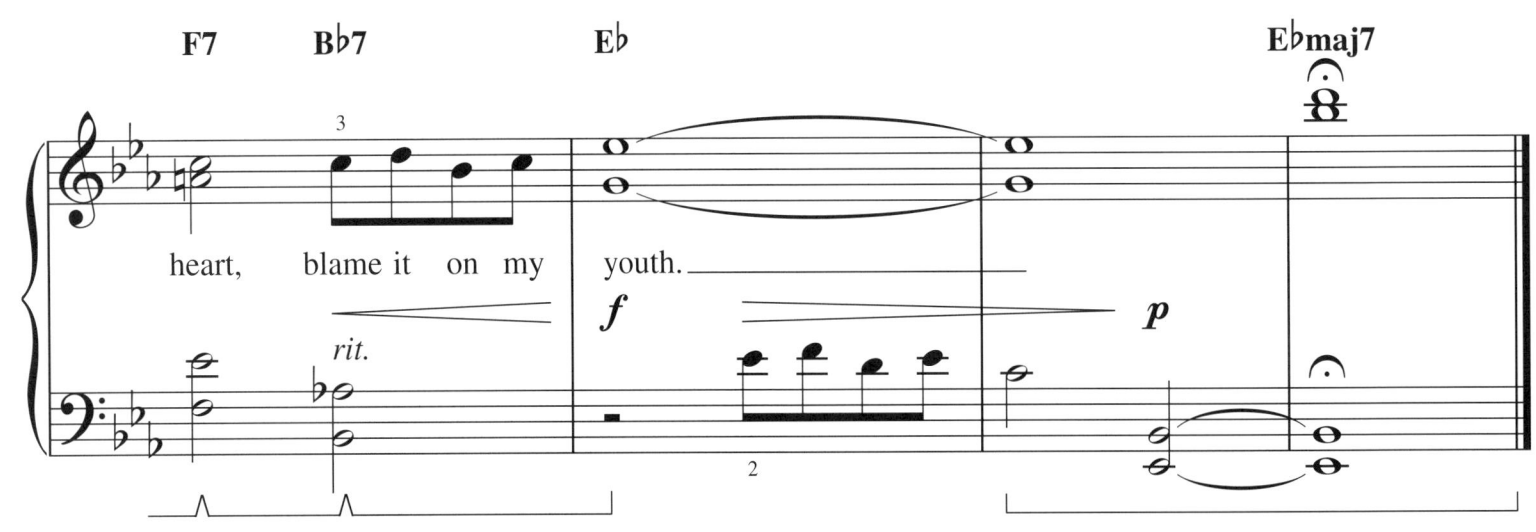

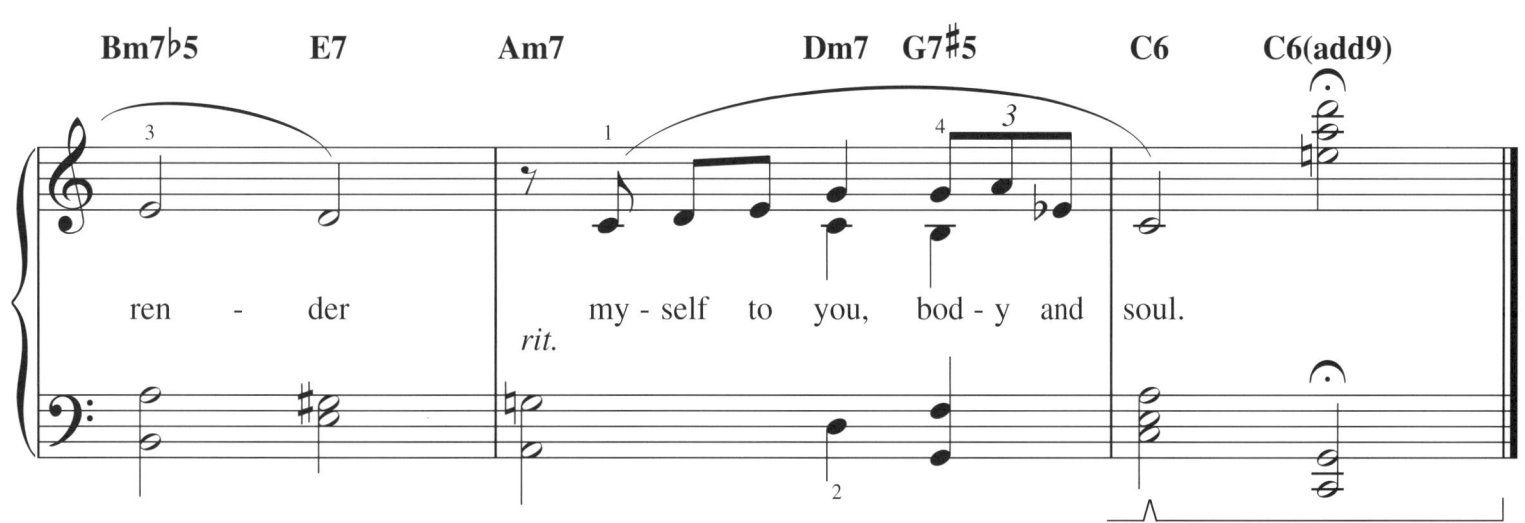

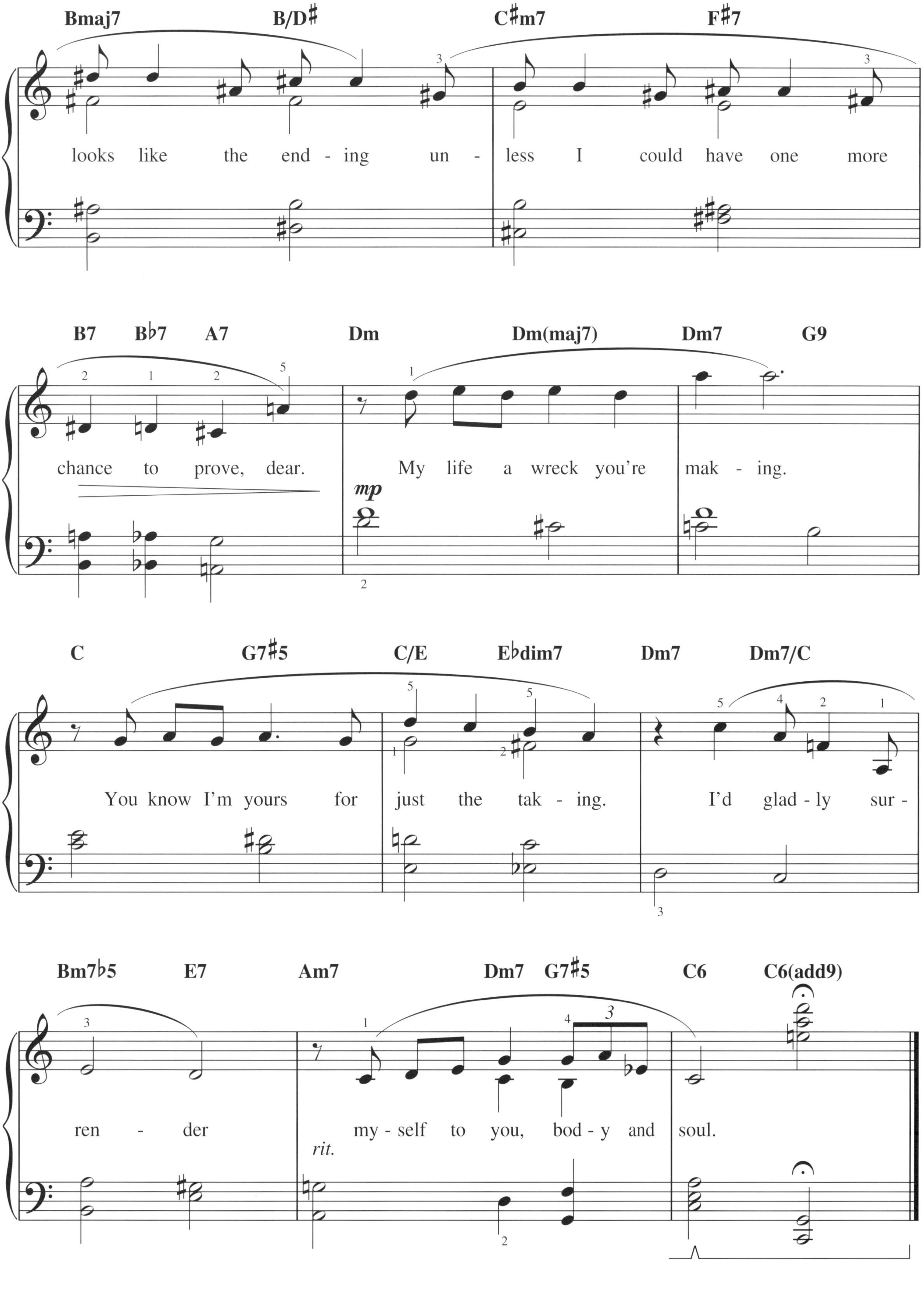
Bmaj7 B/D♯ C♯m7 F♯7
looks like the end - ing un - less I could have one more
B7 B♭7 A7 Dm Dm(maj7) Dm7 G9
chance to prove, dear. My life a wreck you're mak - ing.
mp
C G7♯5 C/E E♭dim7 Dm7 Dm7/C
You know I'm yours for just the tak - ing. I'd glad - ly sur -
Bm7♭5 E7 Am7 Dm7 G7♯5 C6 C6(add9)
ren - der my - self to you, bod - y and soul.
rit.

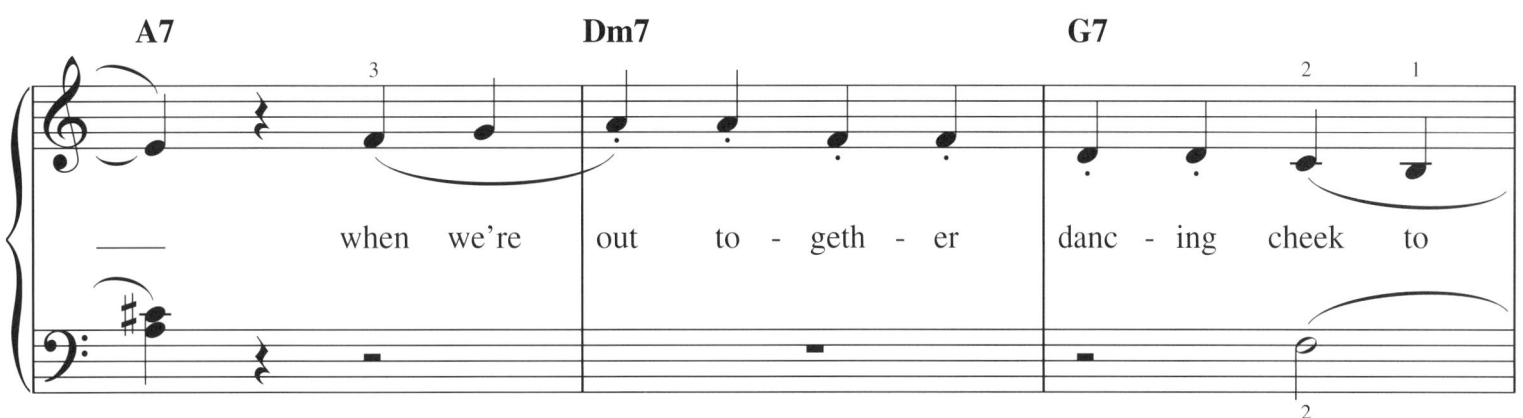
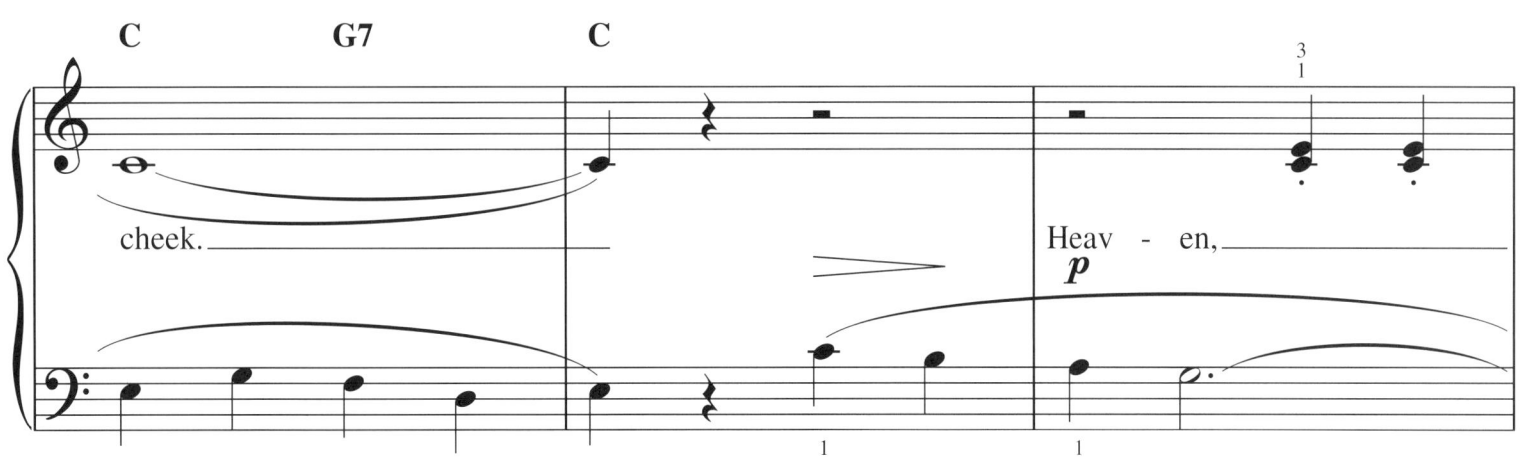
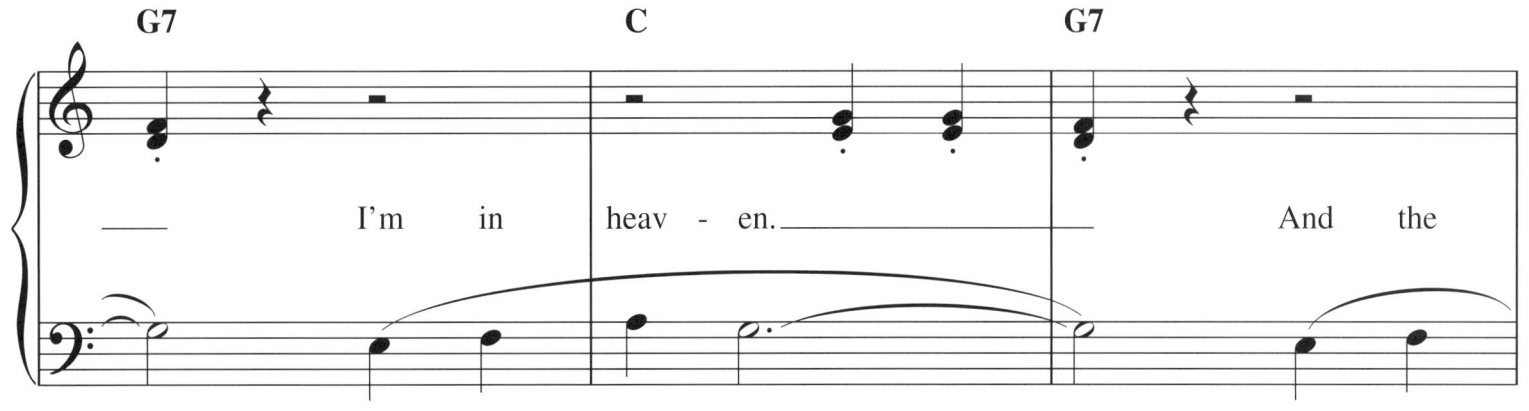

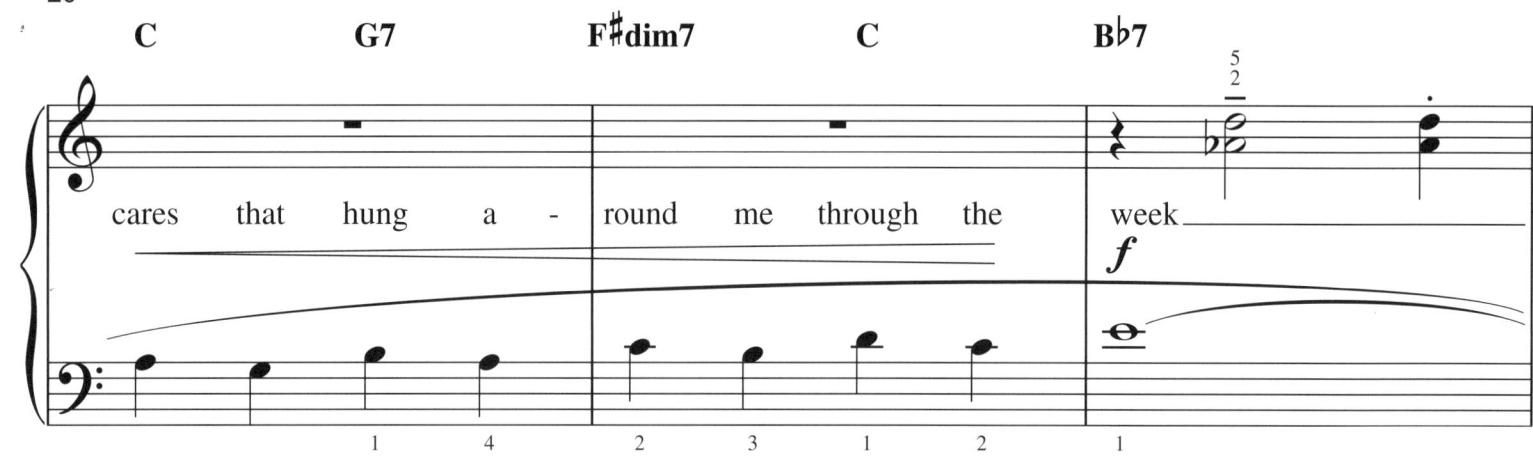
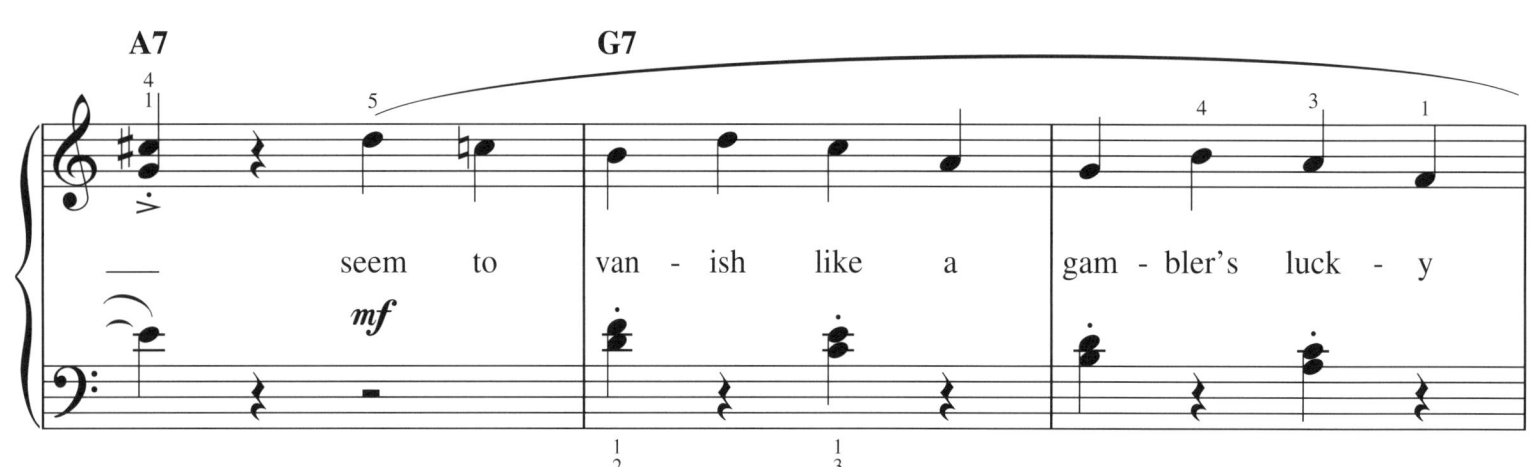
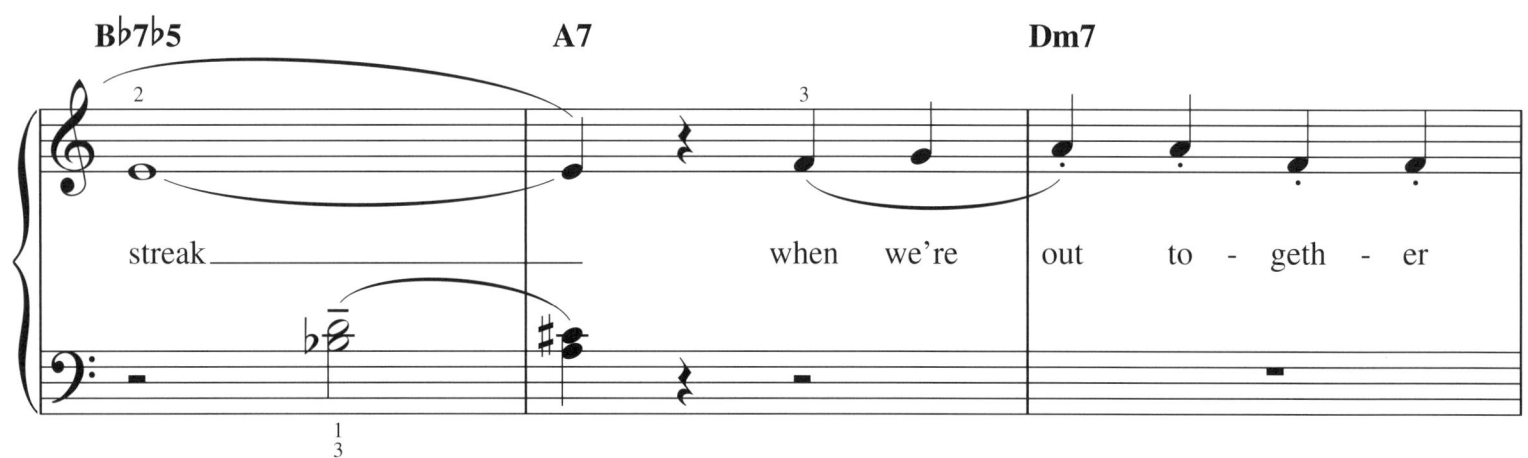
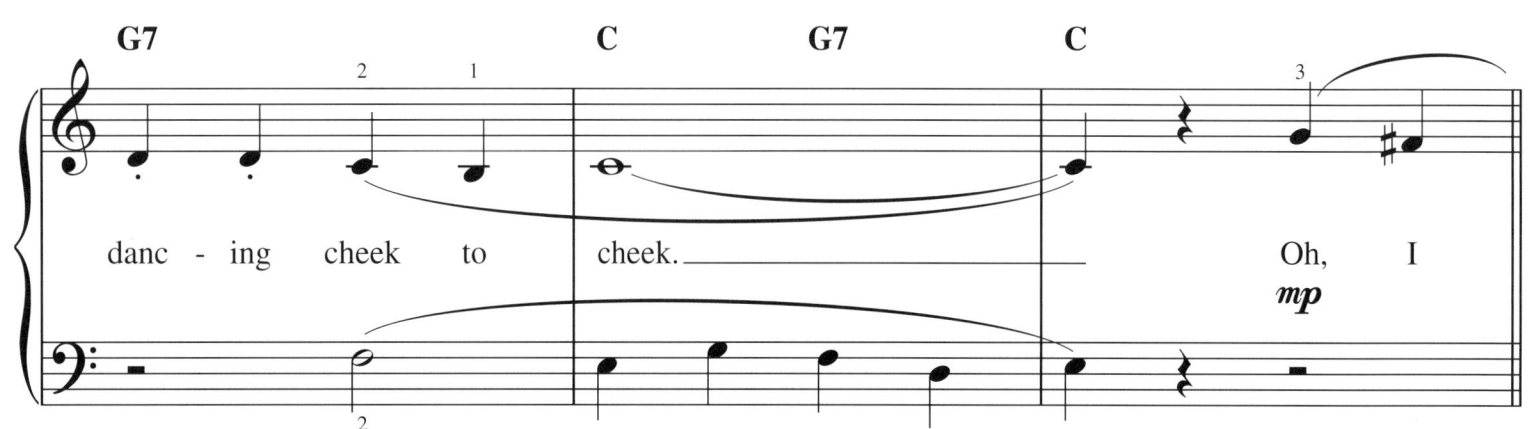

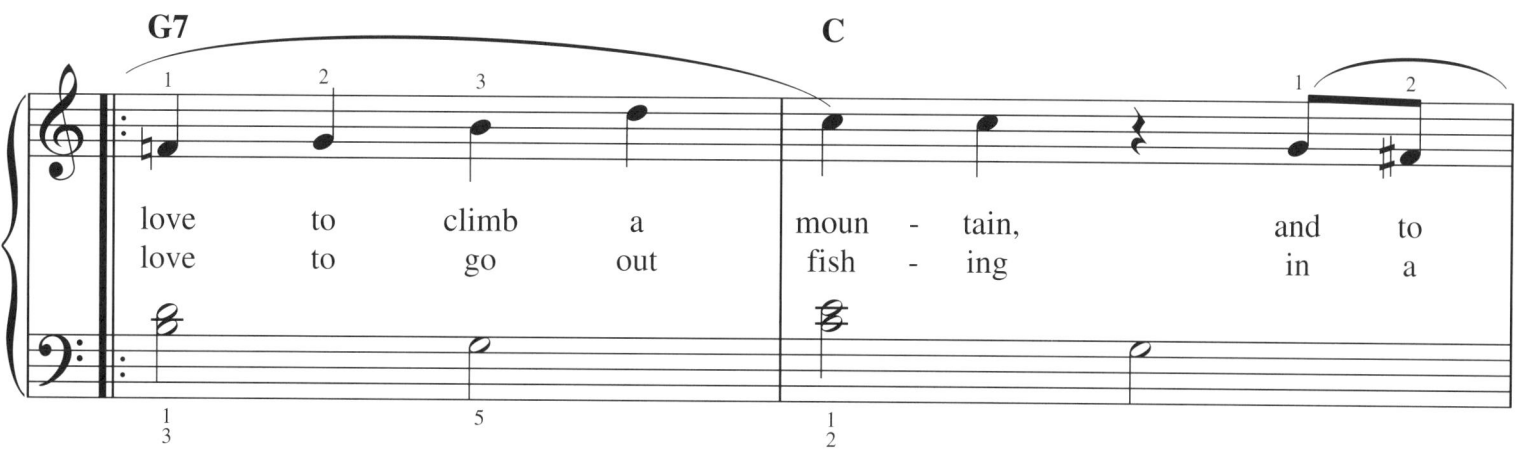
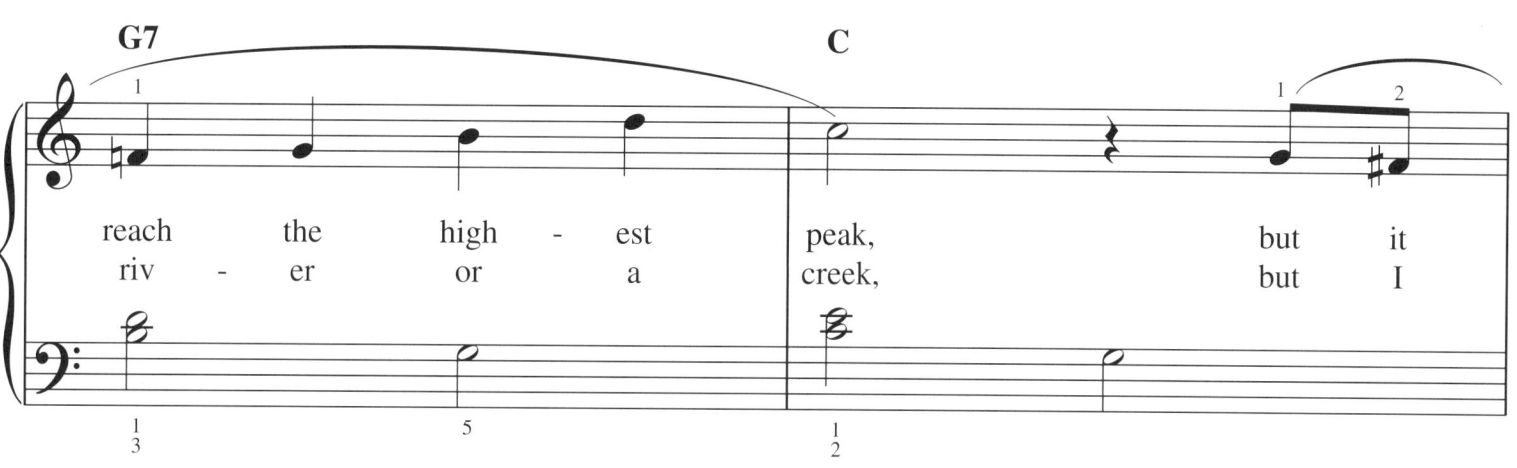
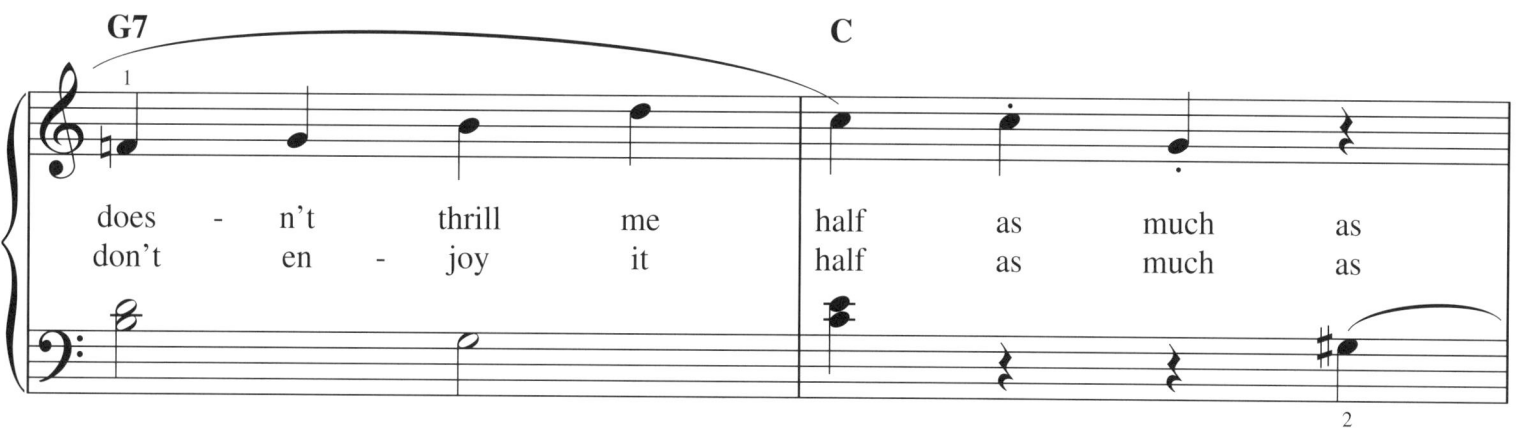
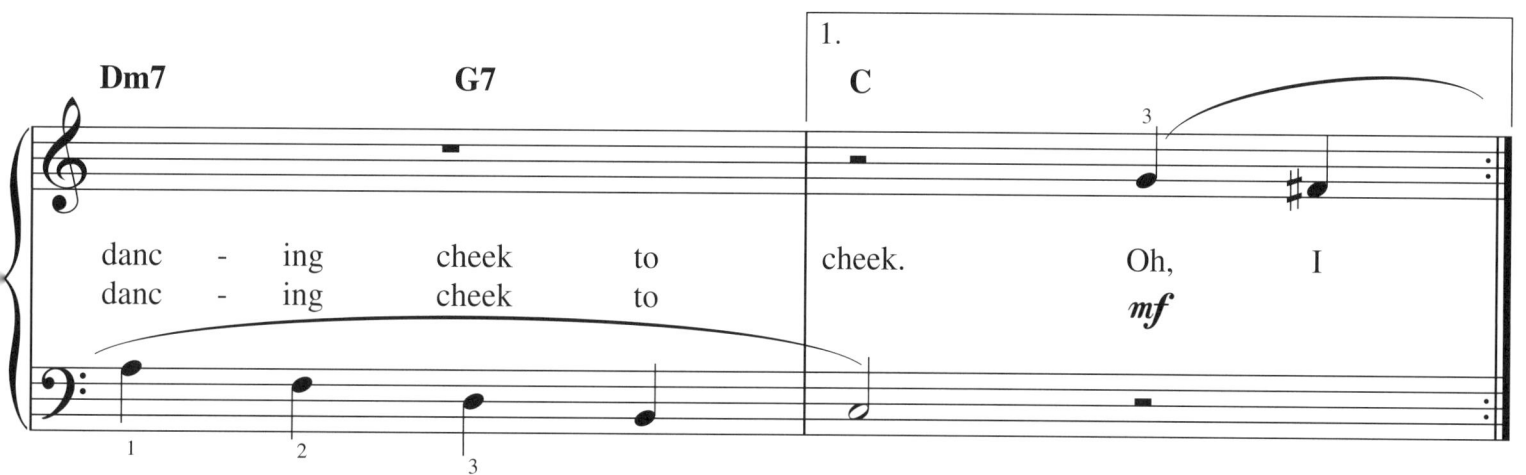

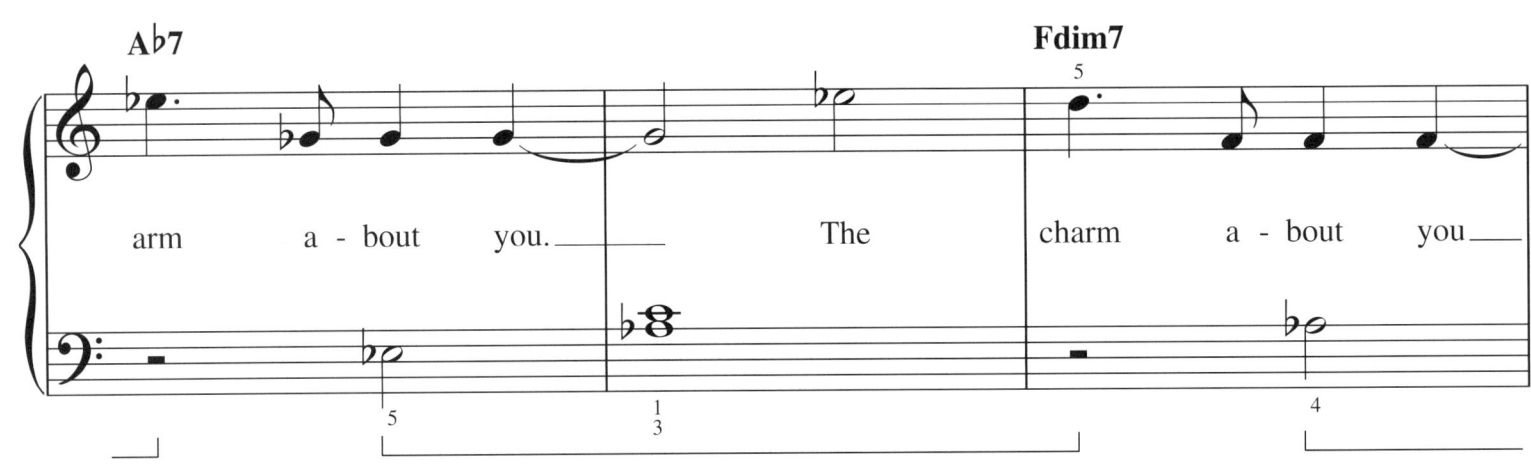
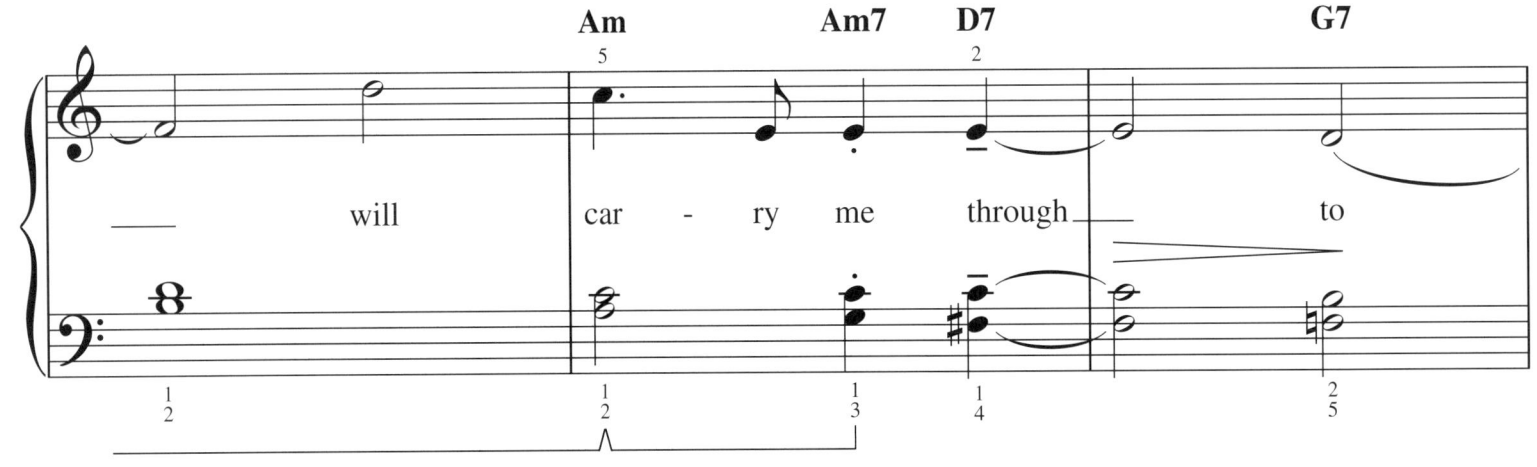
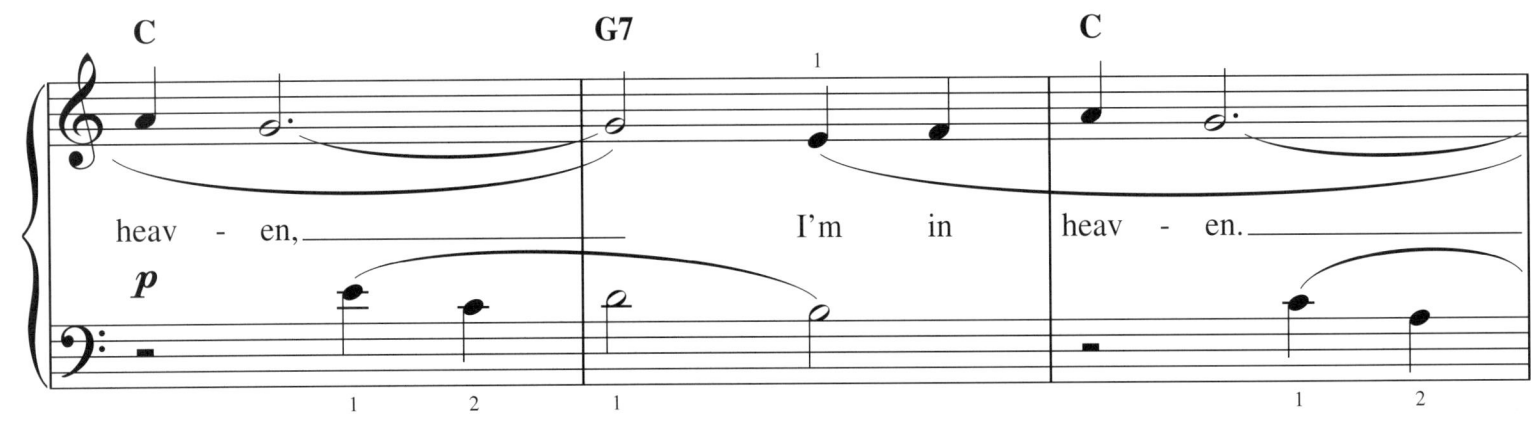

HERE'S THAT RAINY DAY
from CARNIVAL IN FLANDERS

Words by JOHNNY BURKE
Music by JIMMY VAN HEUSEN
Arranged by Phillip Keveren

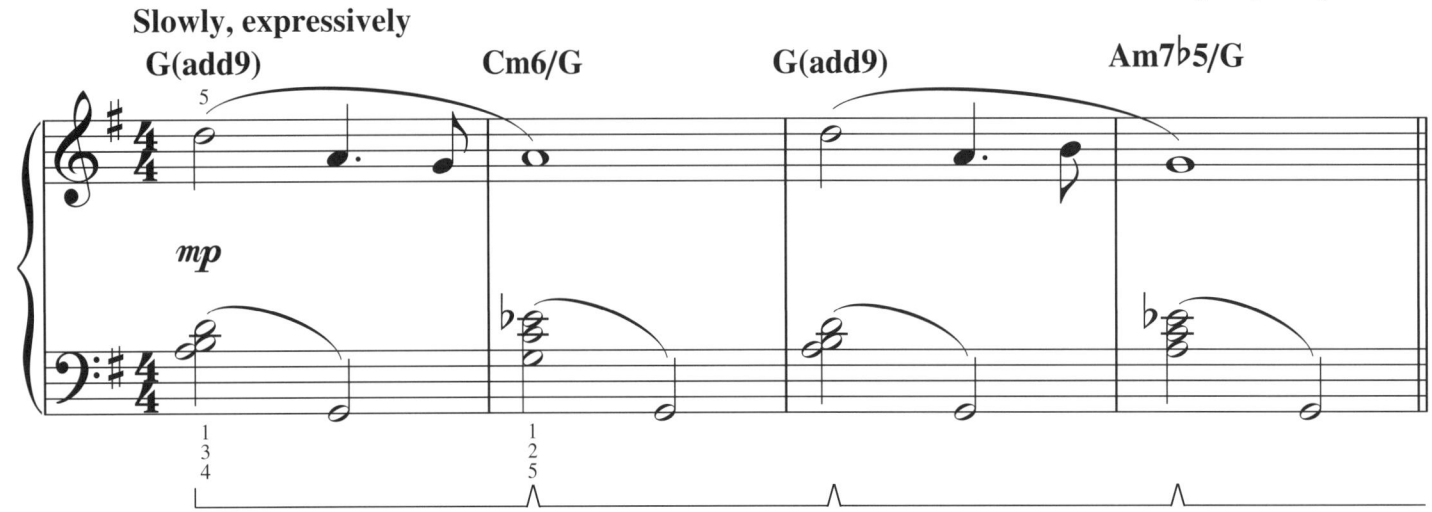

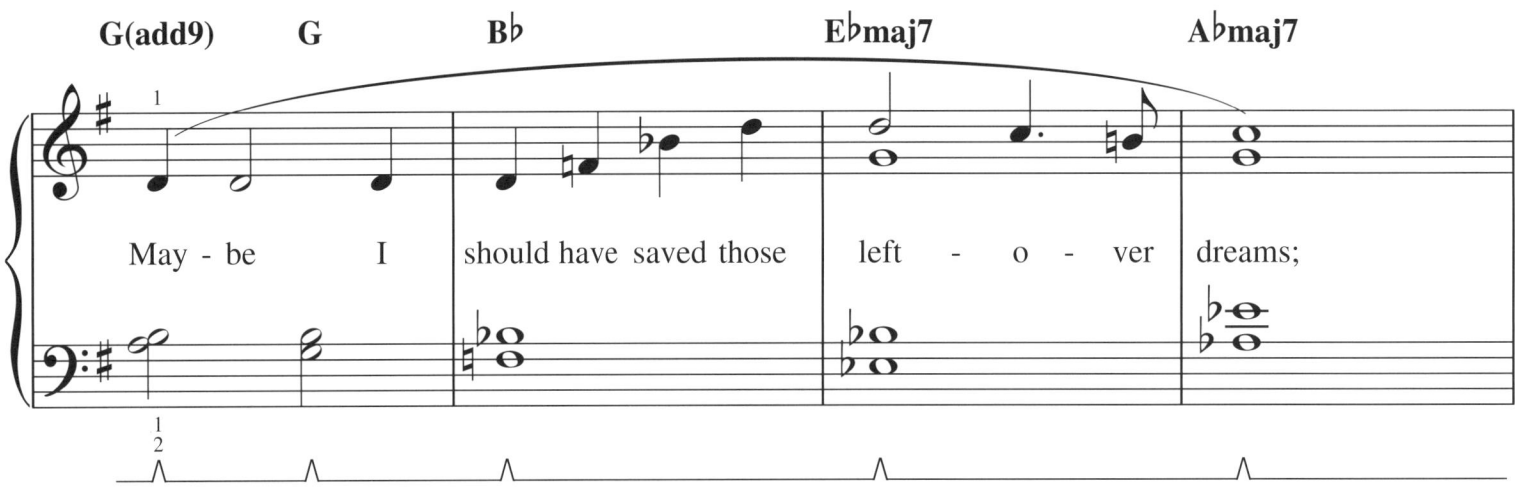

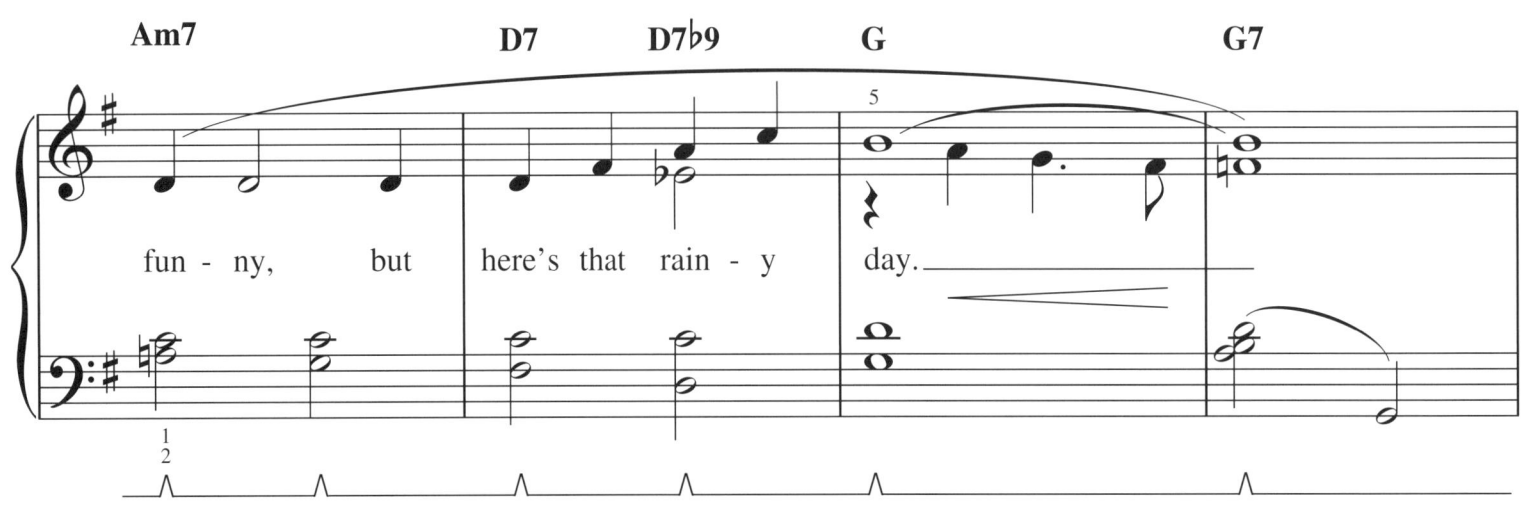

Copyright © 1949 by Bourne Co. and Dorsey Bros. Music, a division of Music Sales Corporation (ASCAP)
Copyright Renewed
International Copyright Secured   All Rights Reserved
Reprinted by Permission

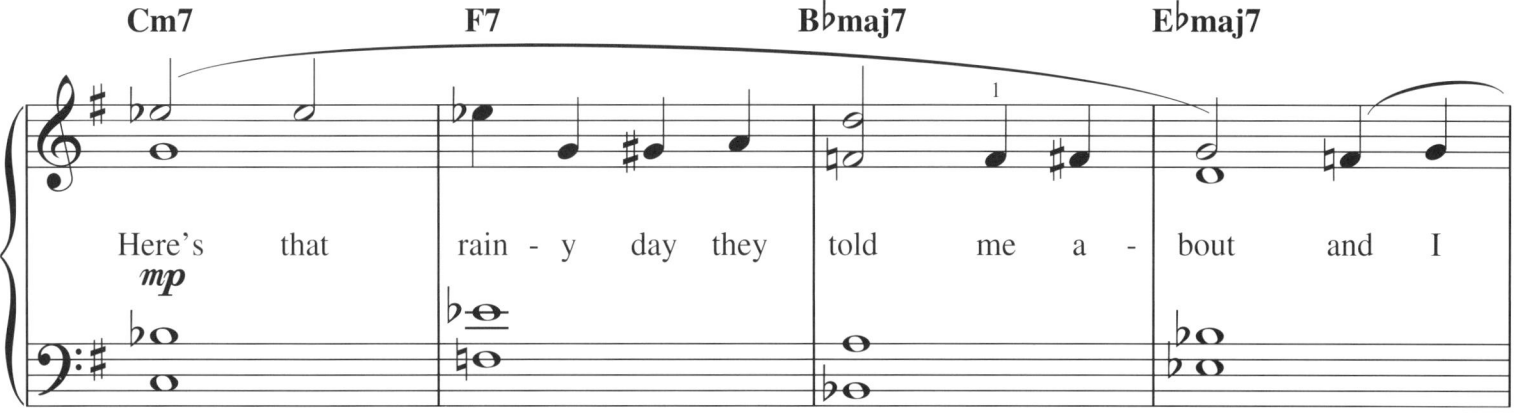

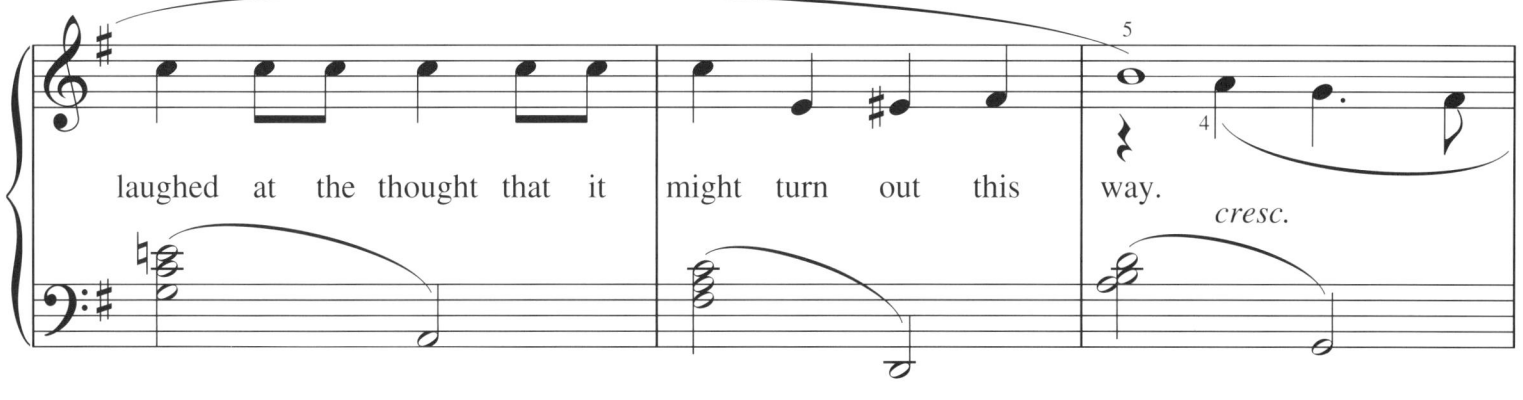
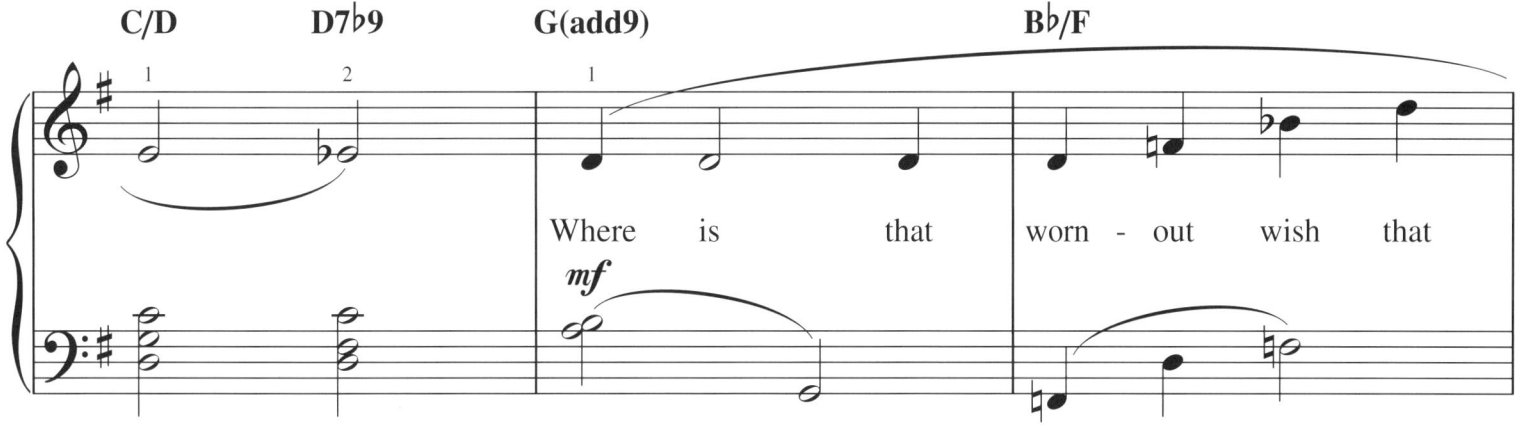
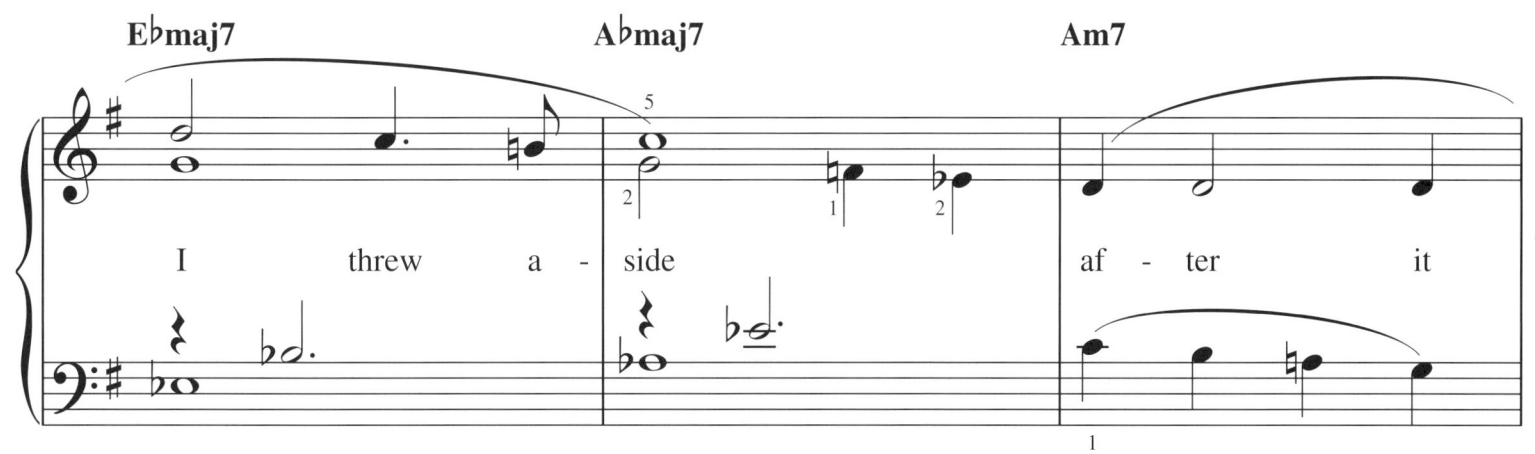

27

I'LL REMEMBER APRIL

Words and Music by PAT JOHNSON,
DON RAYE and GENE DE PAUL
Arranged by Phillip Keveren

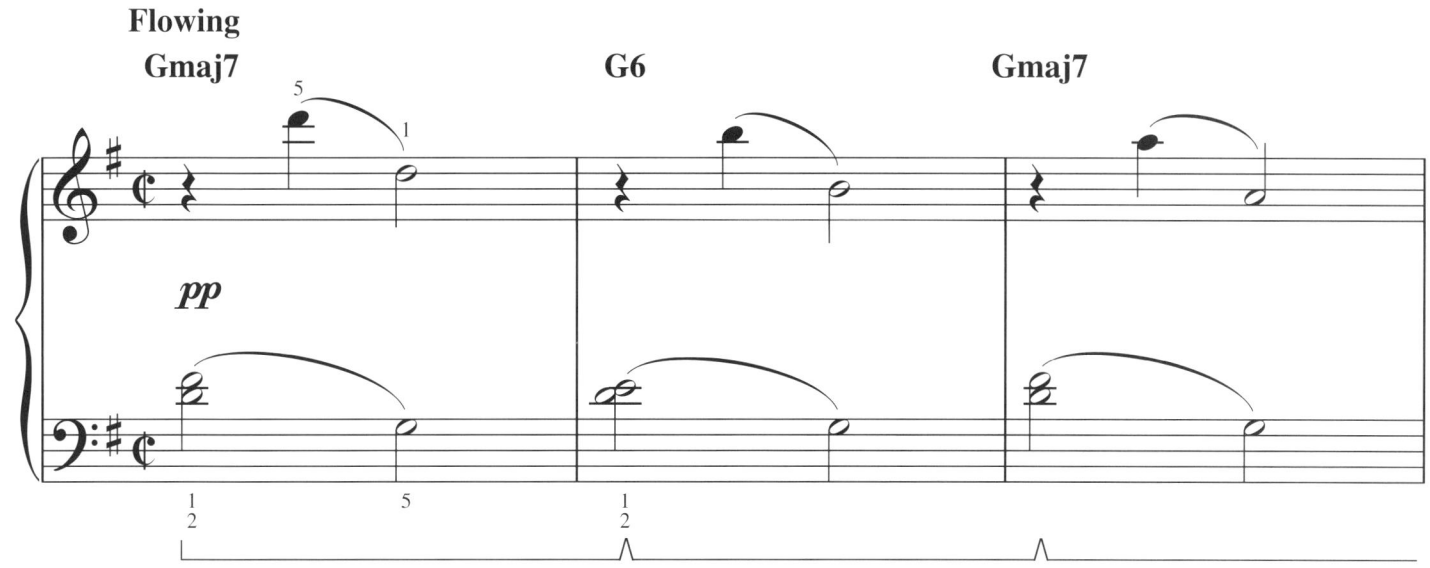

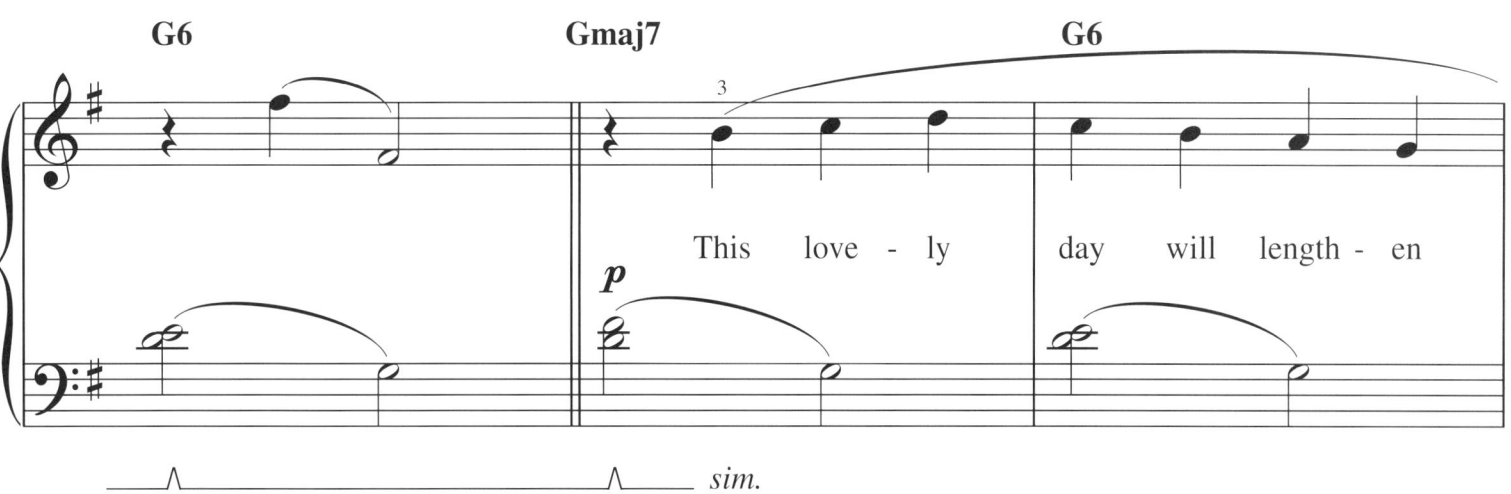

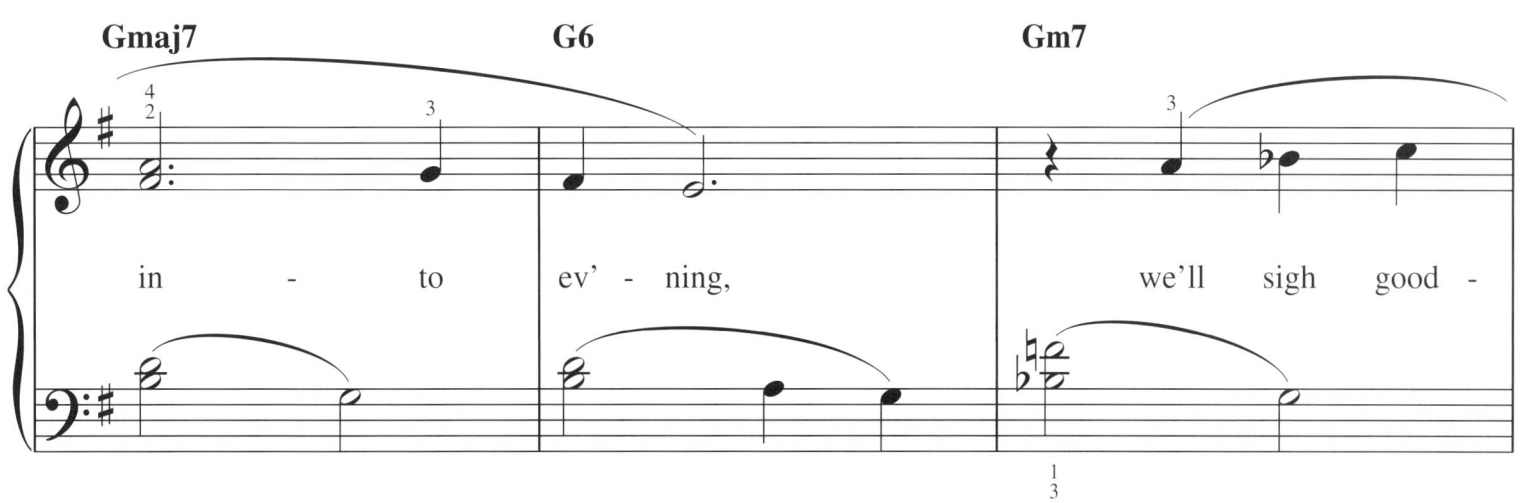

© 1941, 1942 (Renewed) PIC CORPORATION and UNIVERSAL MUSIC CORP.
All Rights Reserved

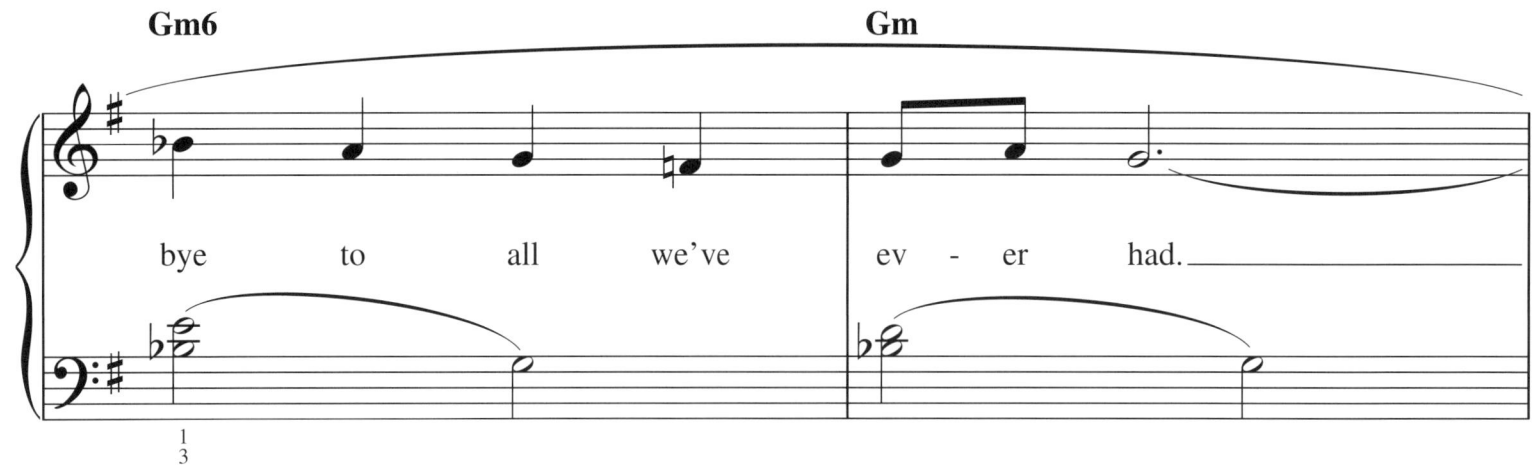
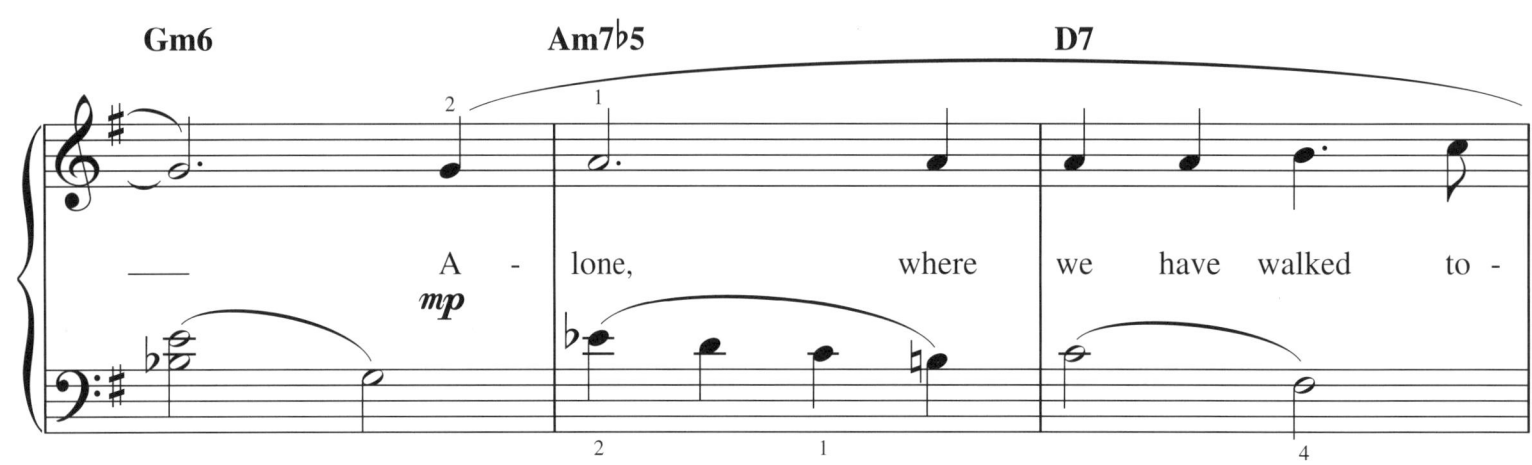
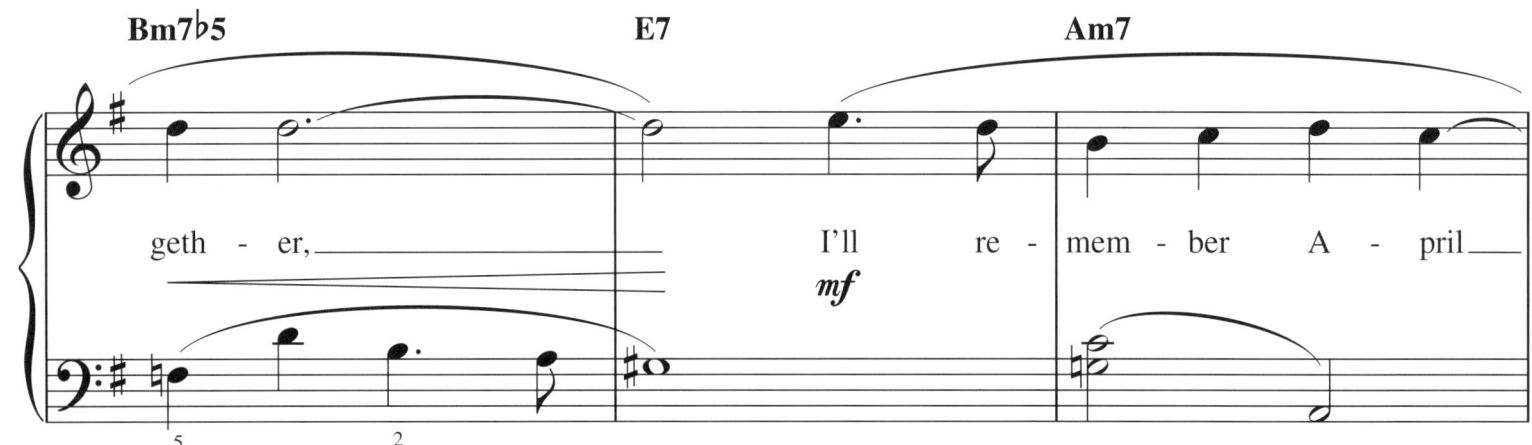
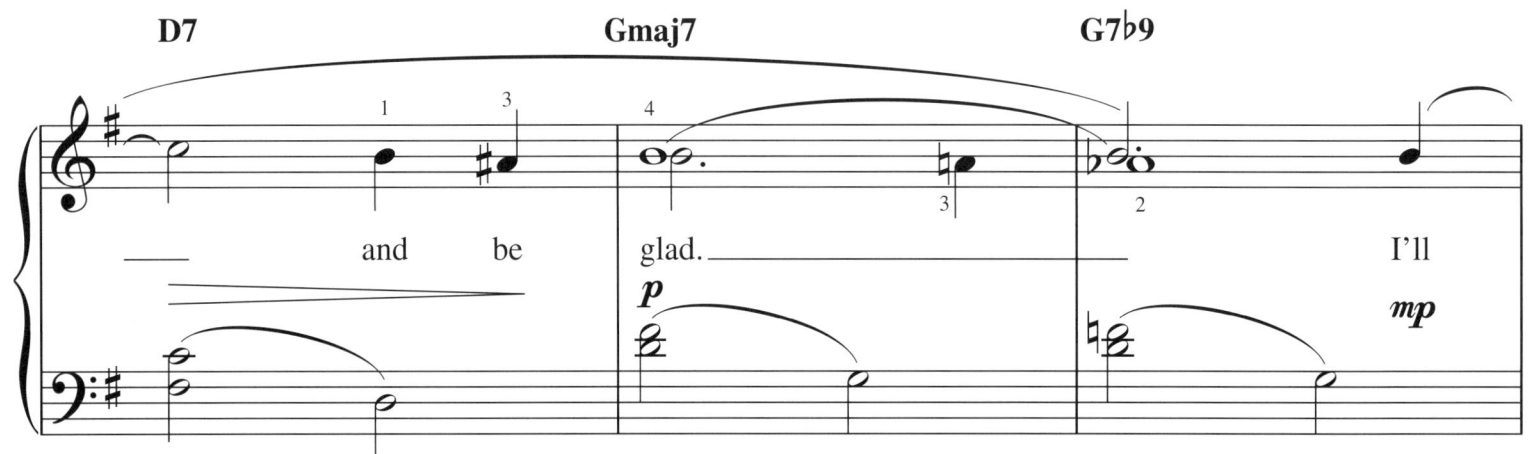

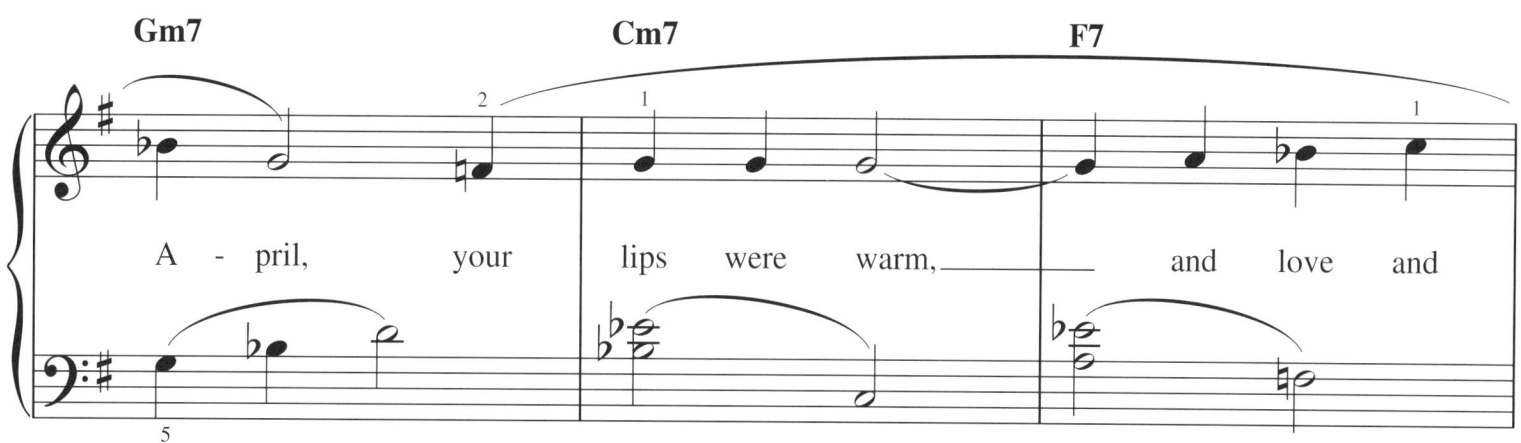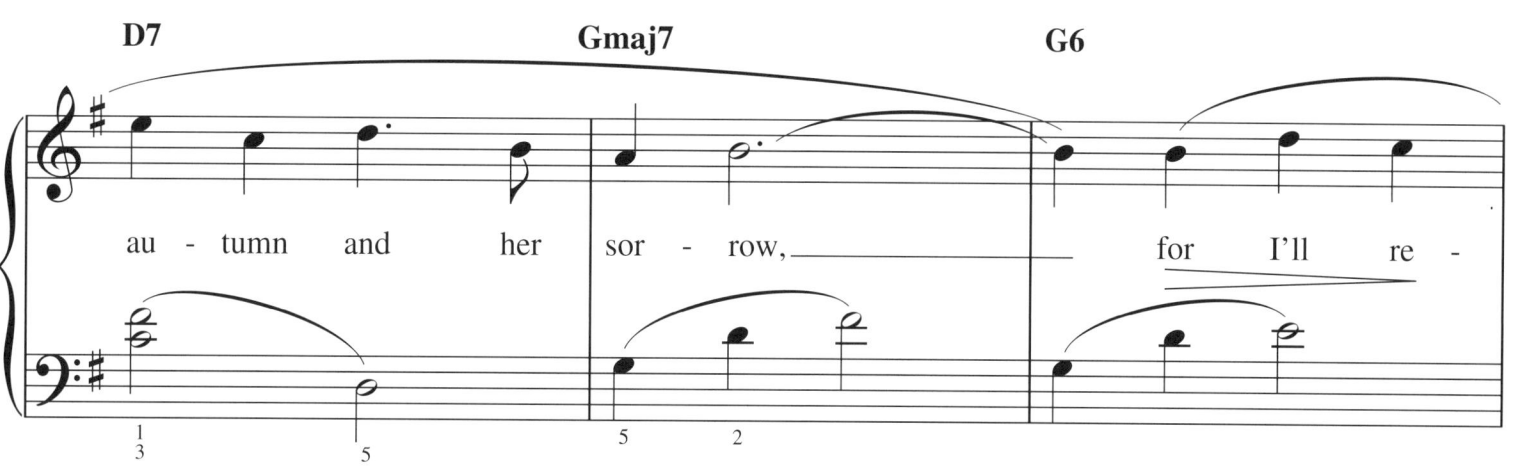

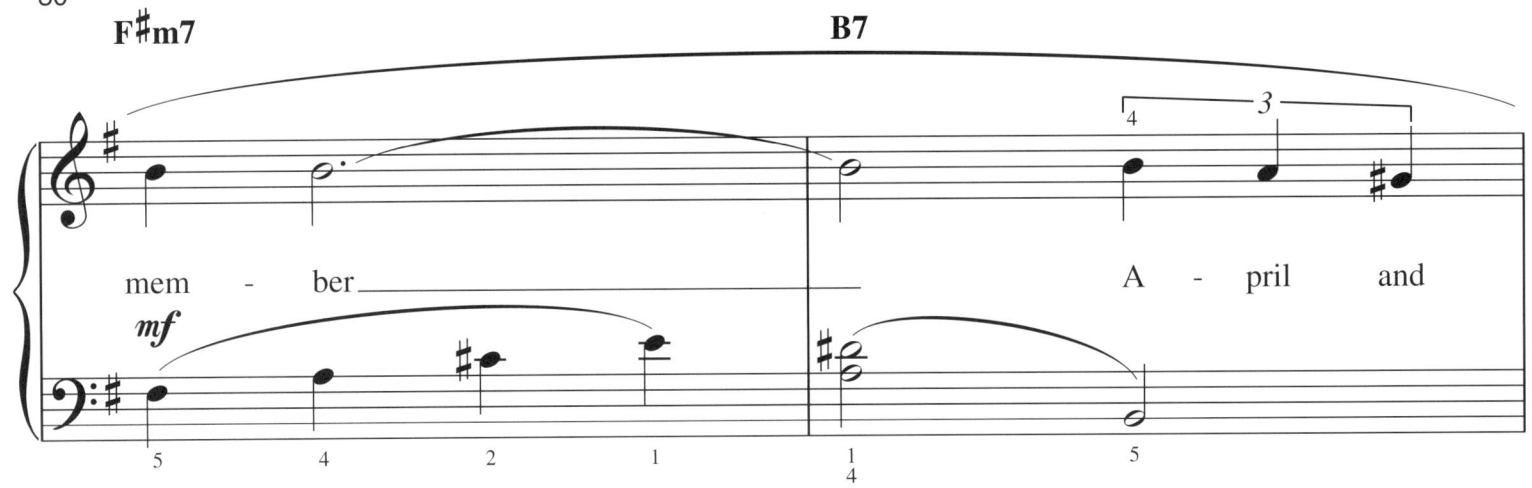
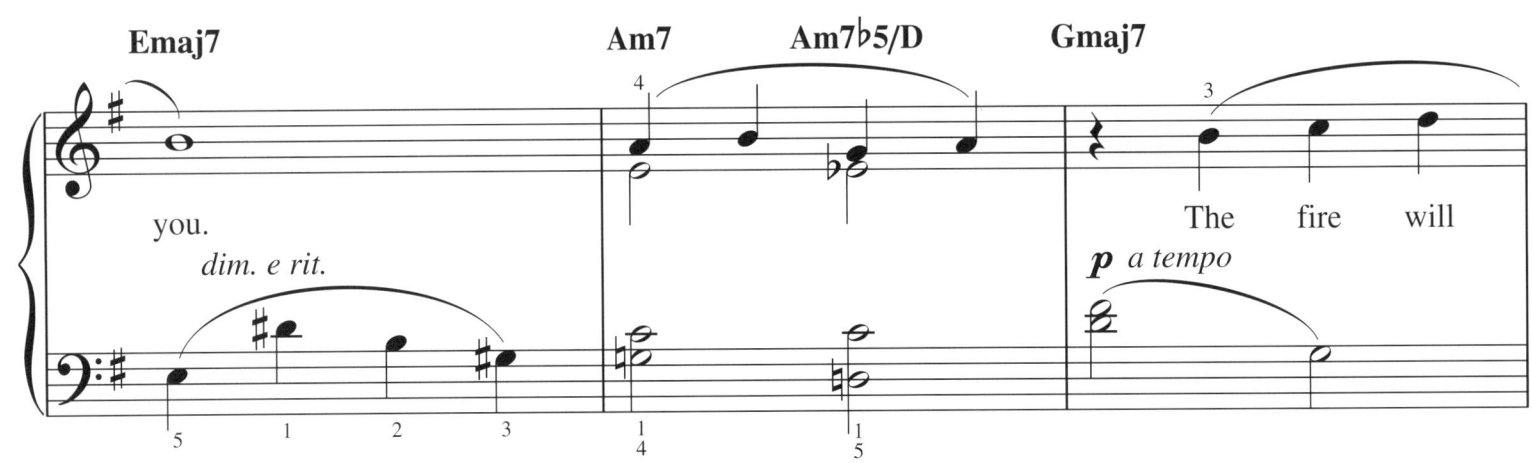
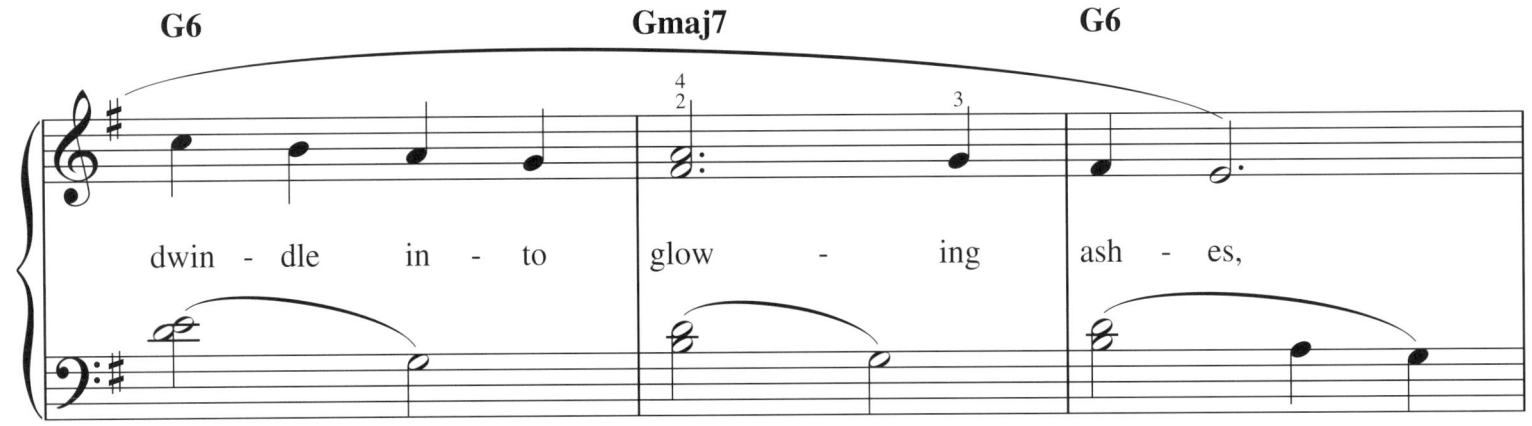

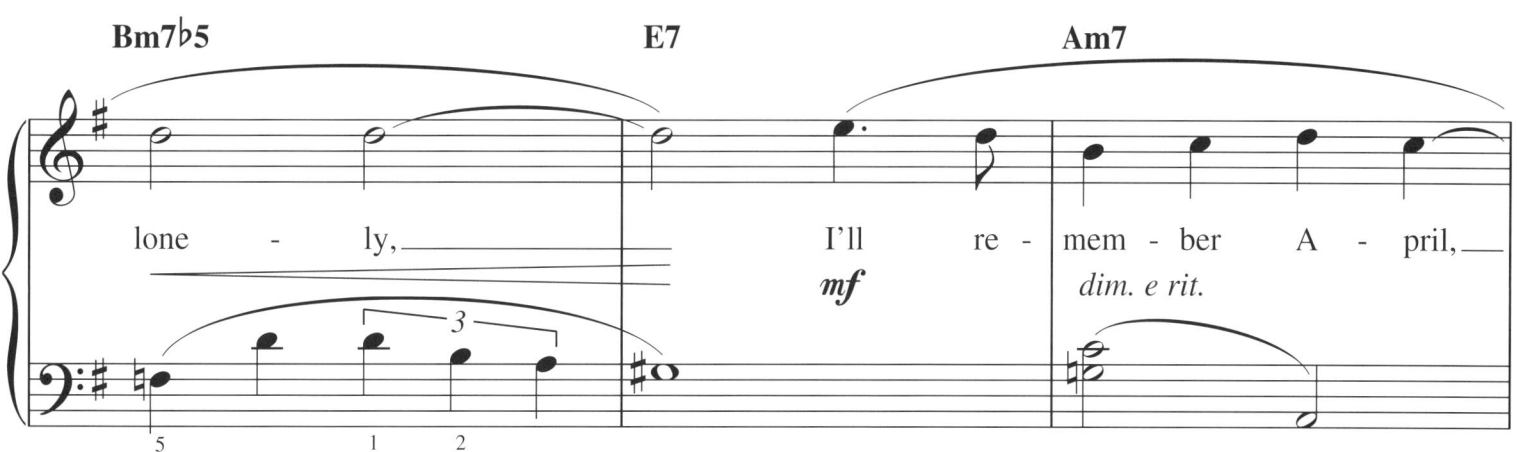
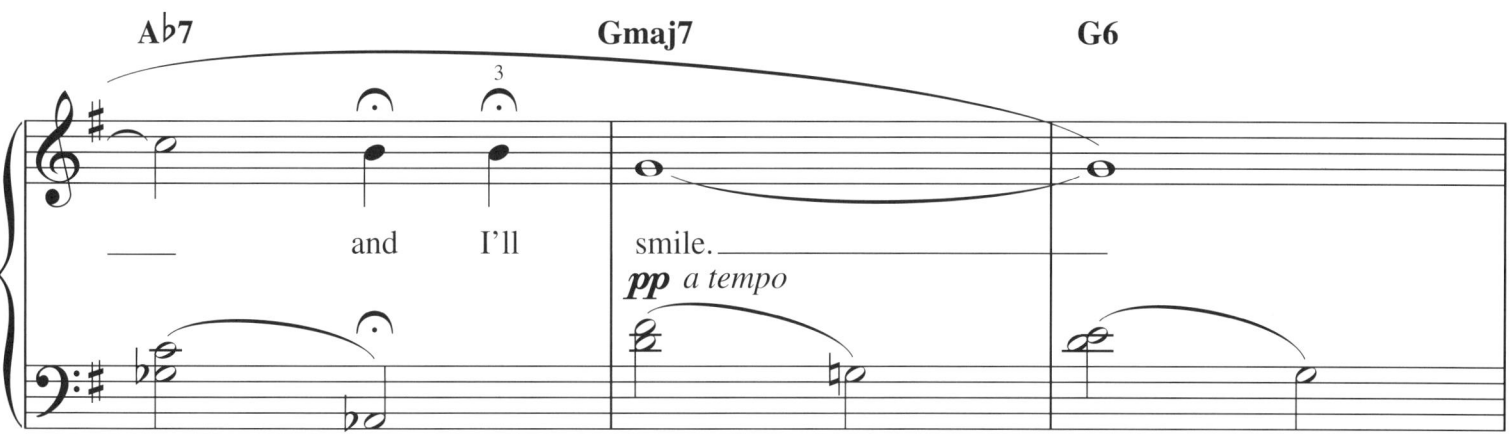
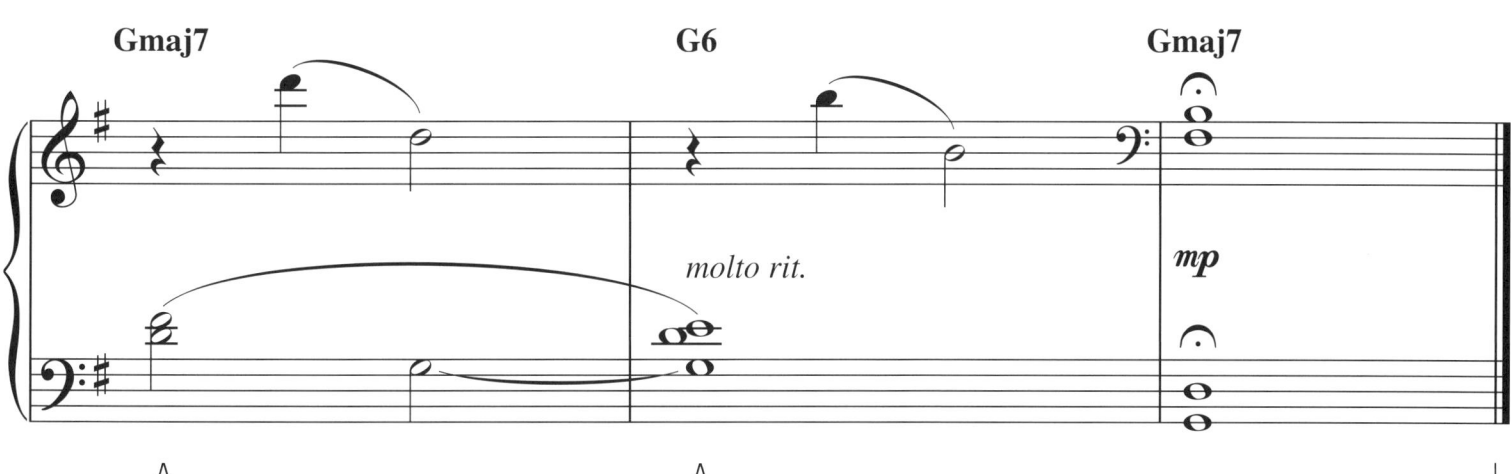

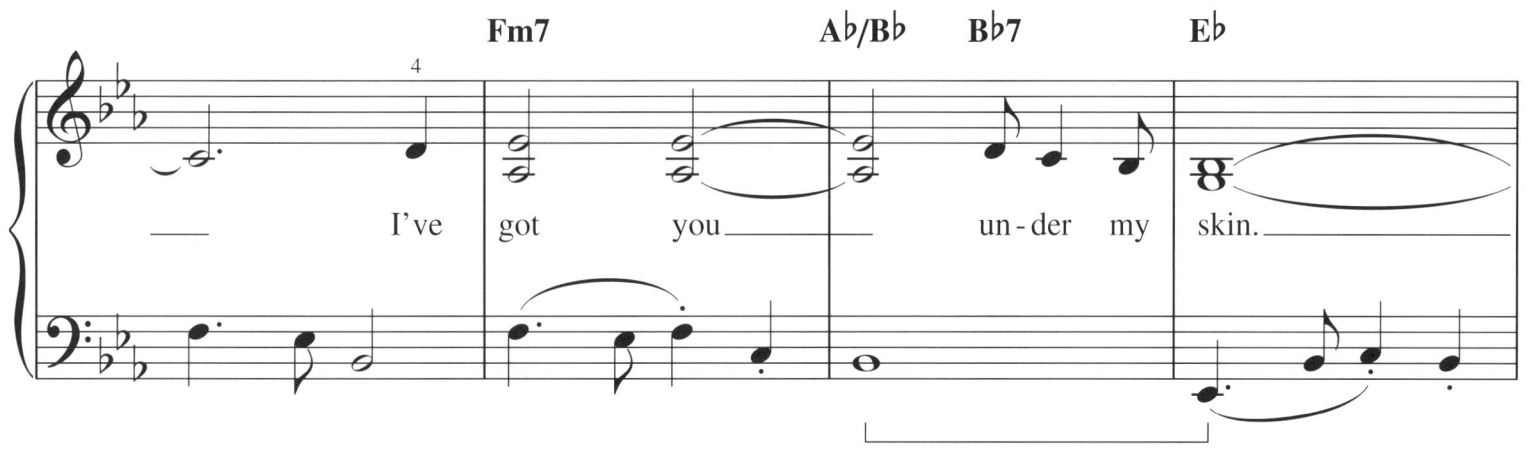
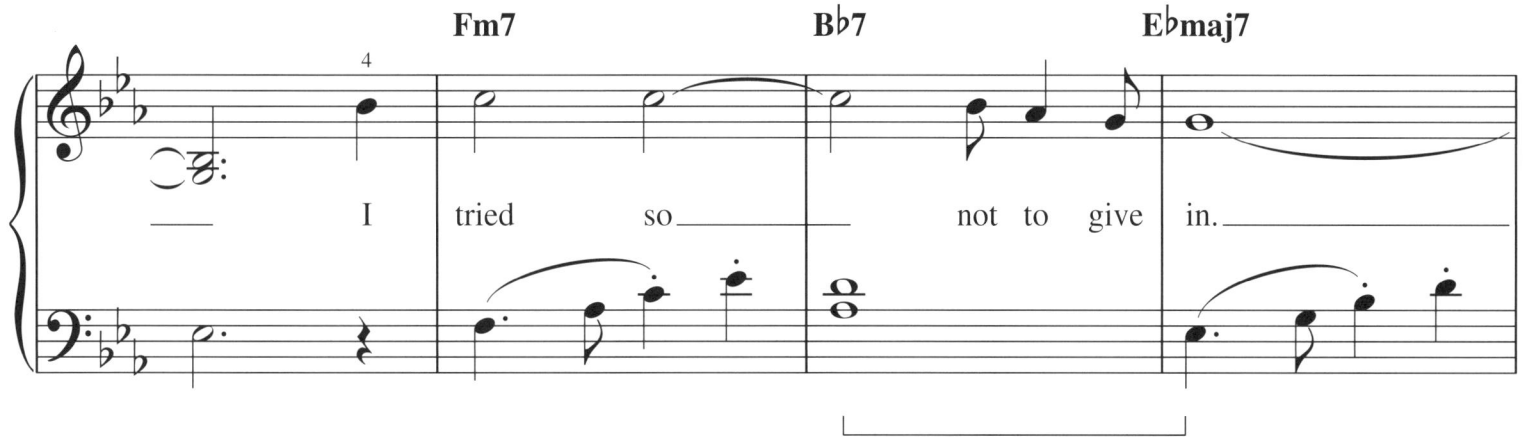
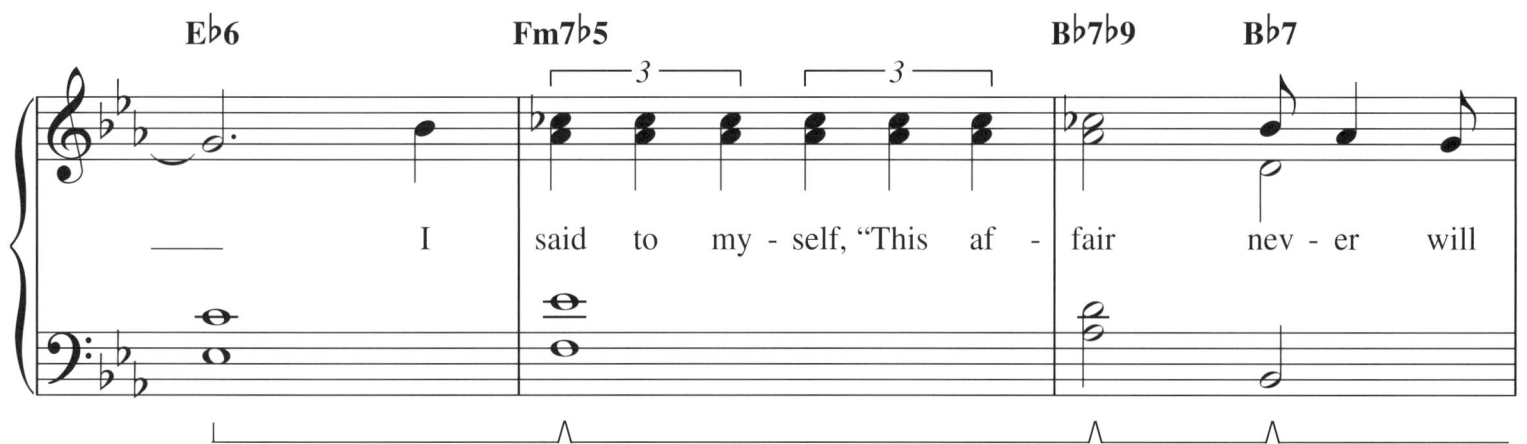

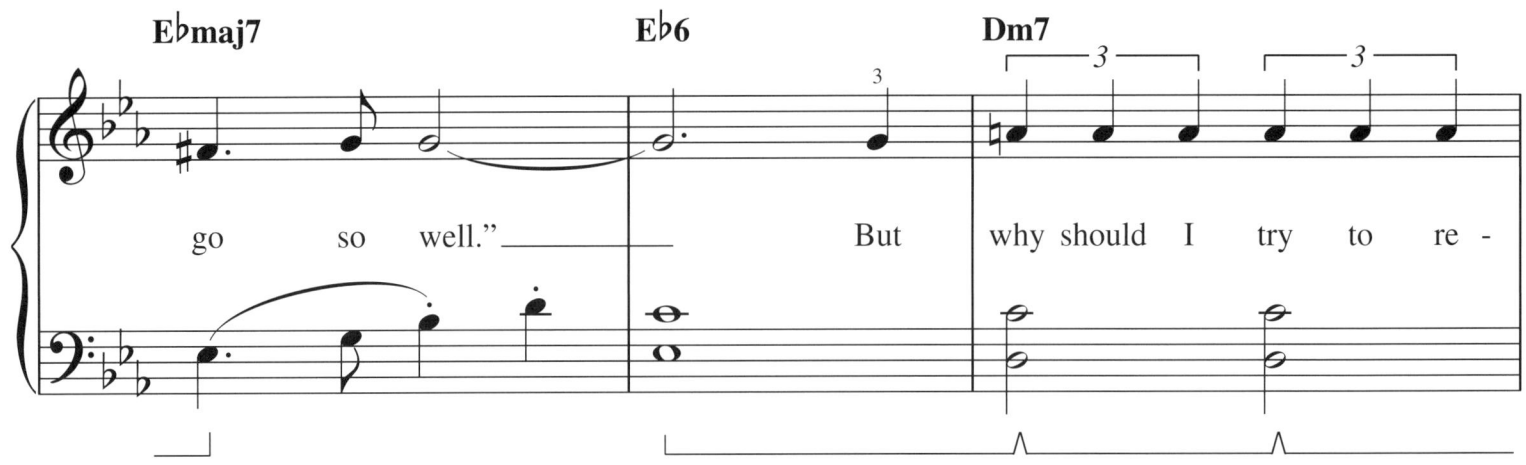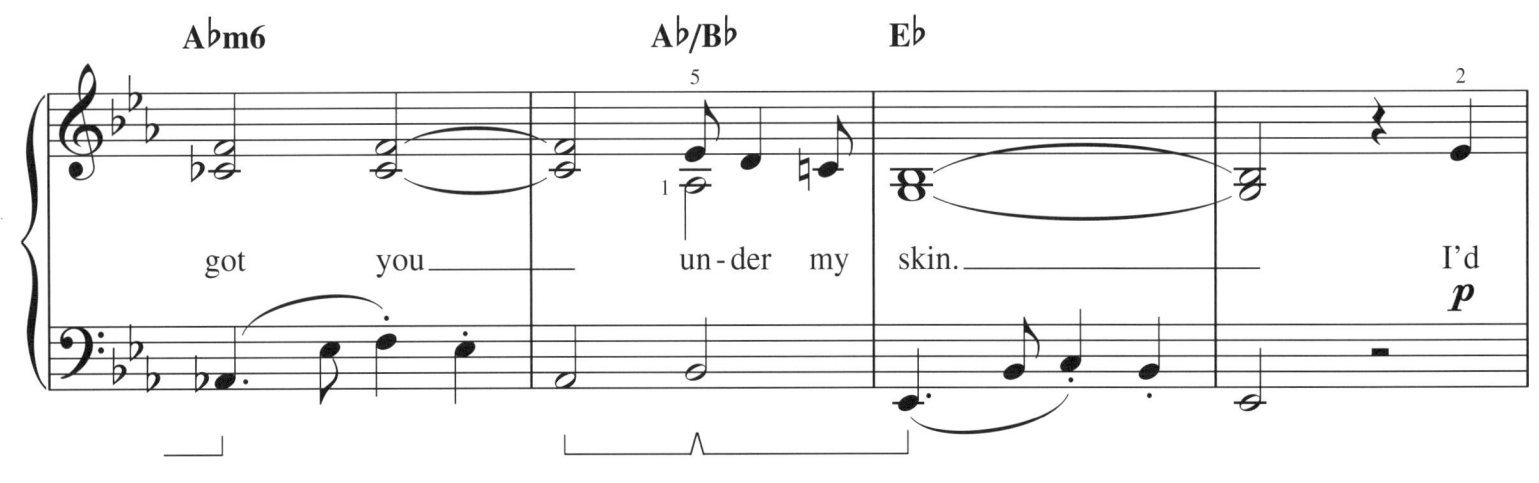

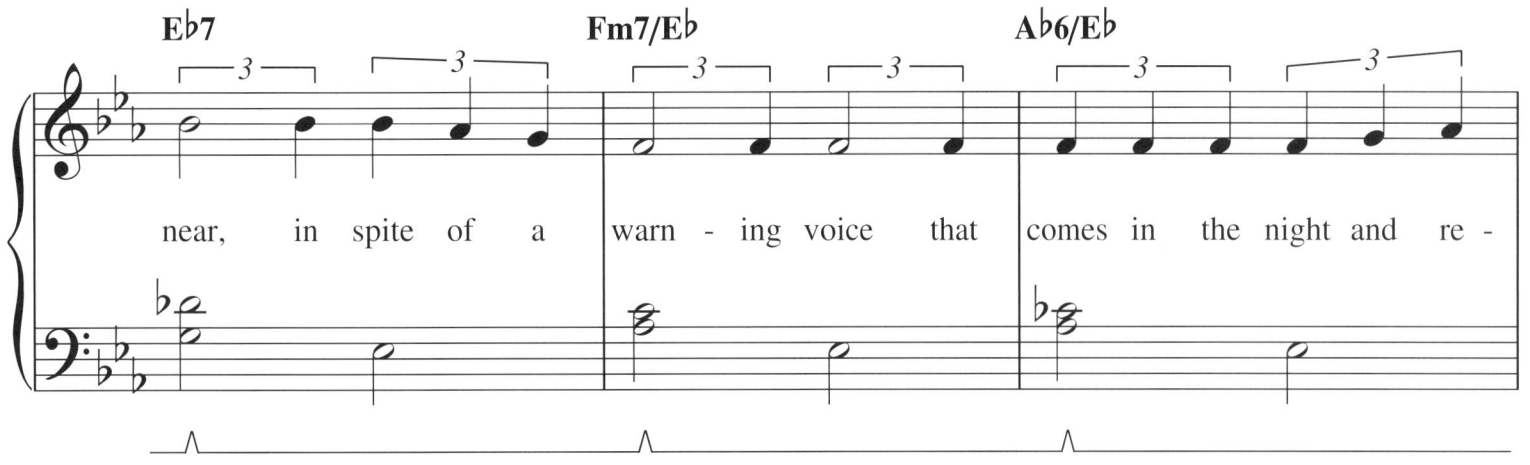

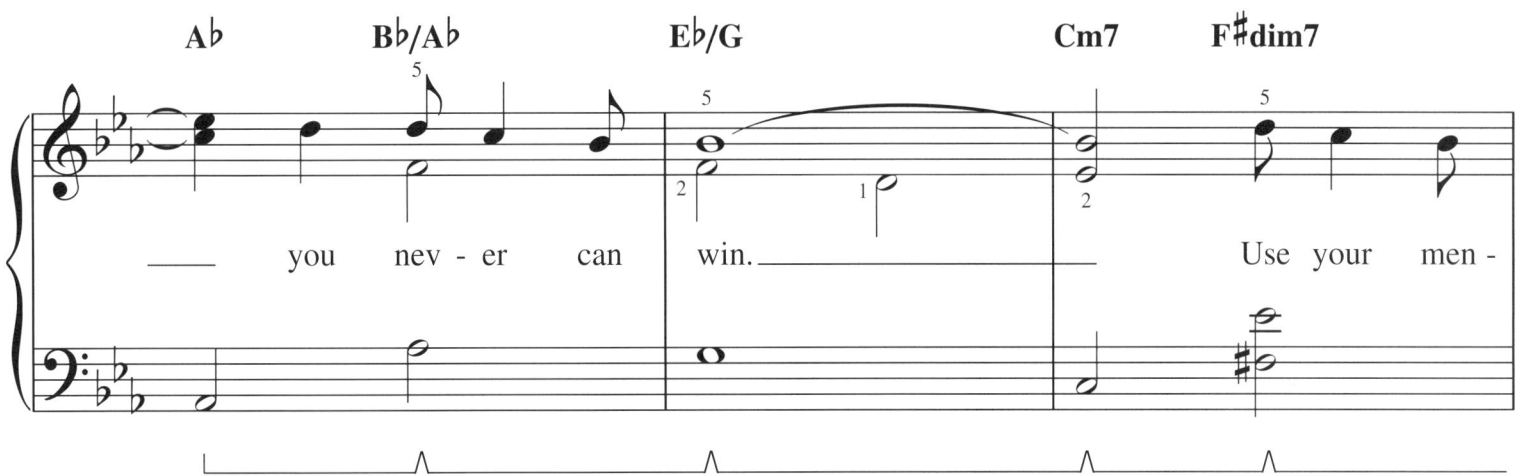
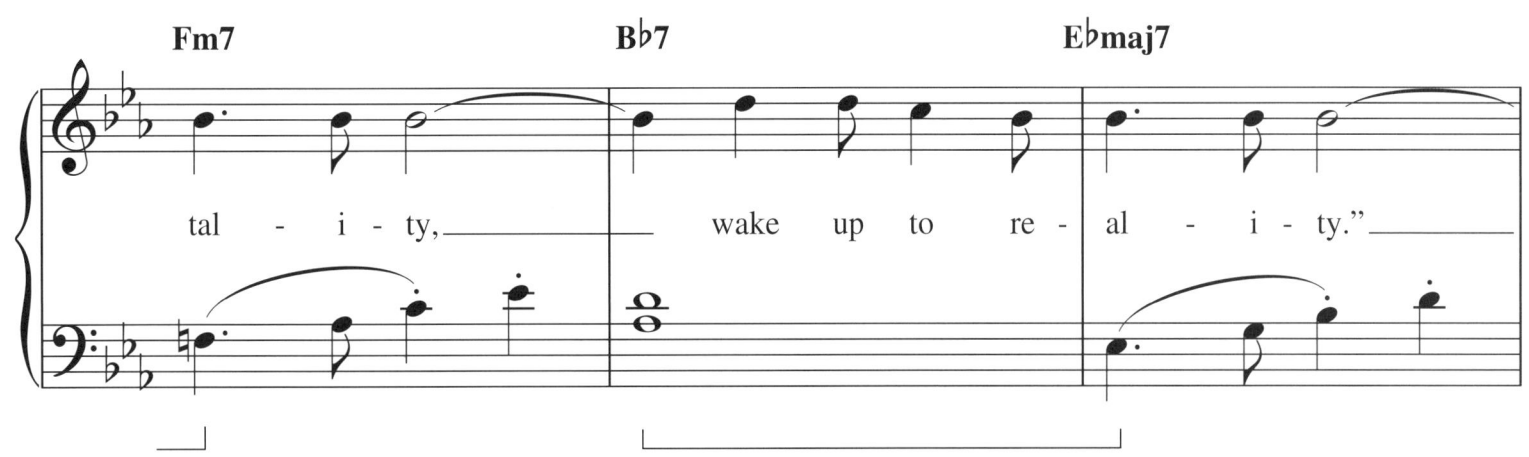

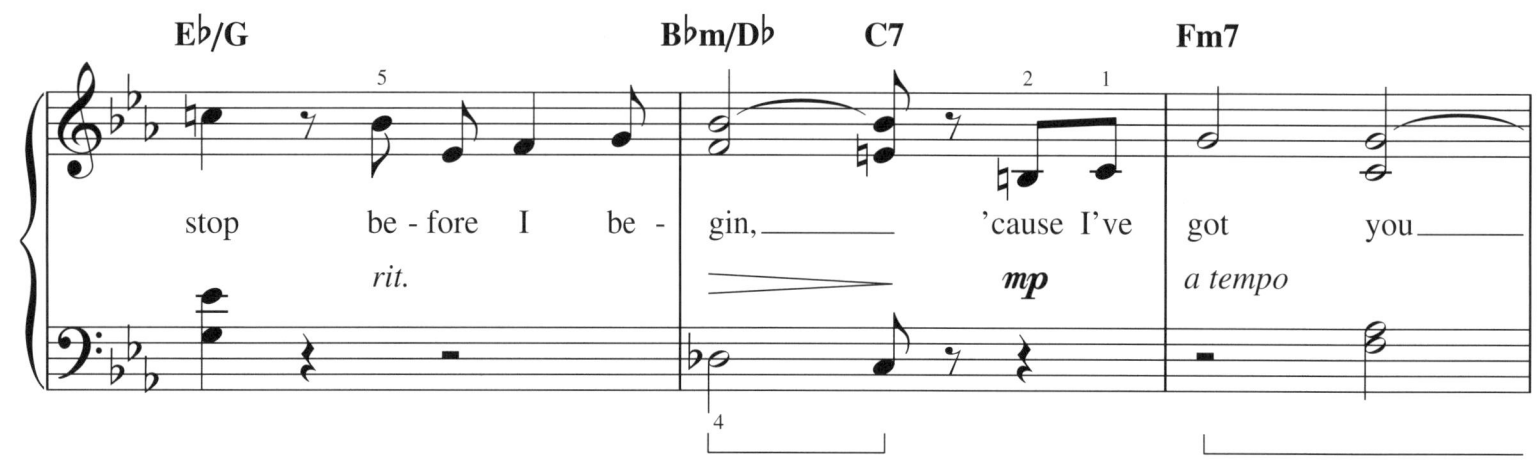
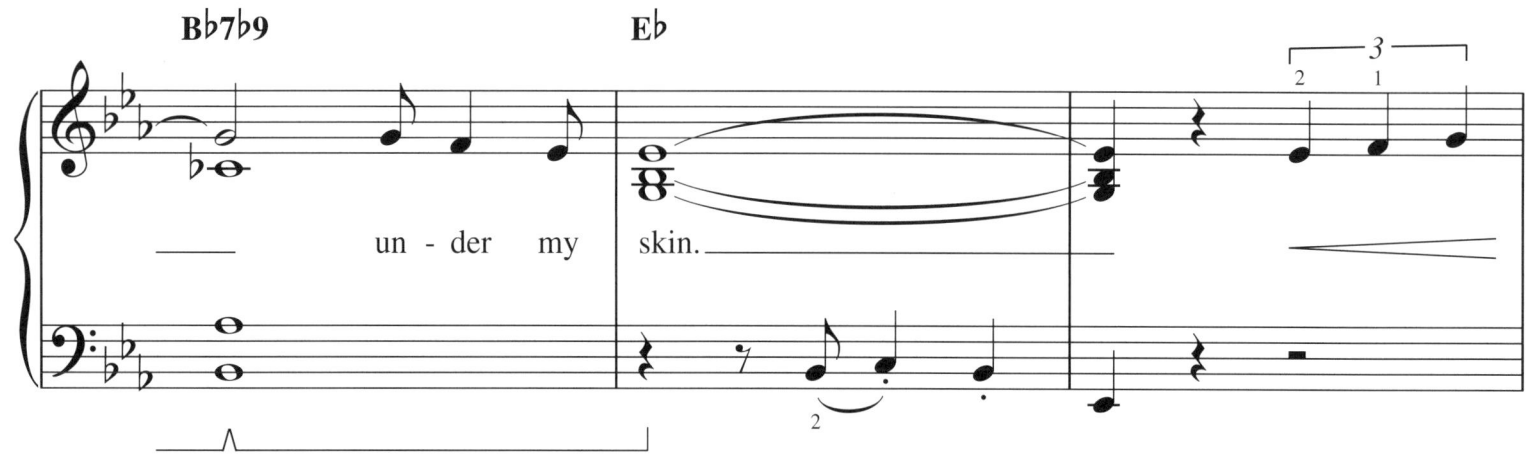
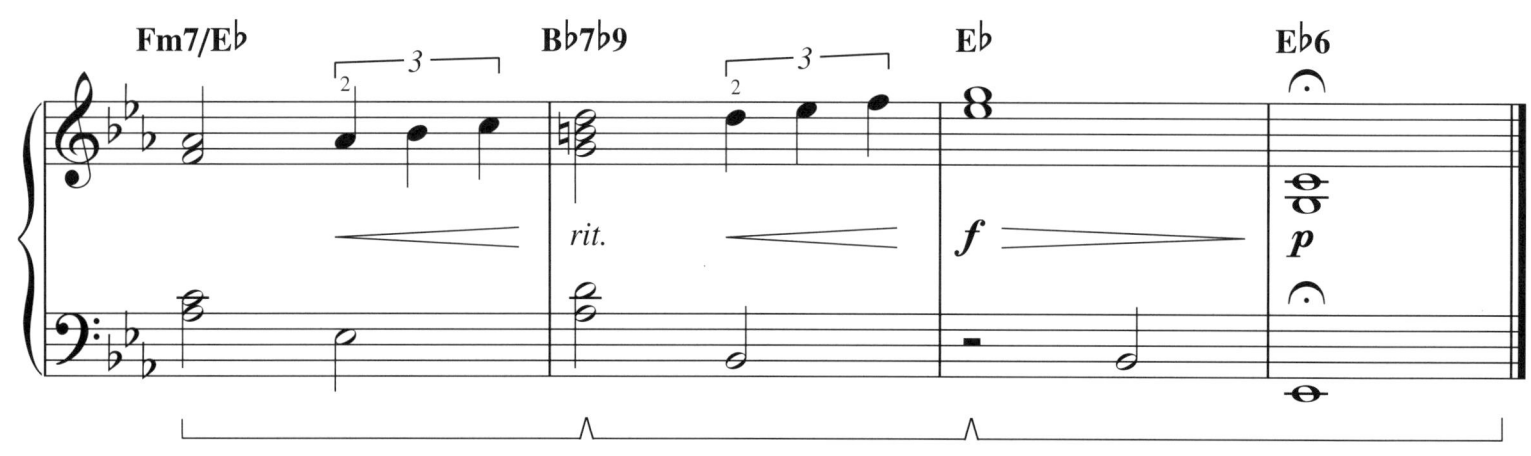

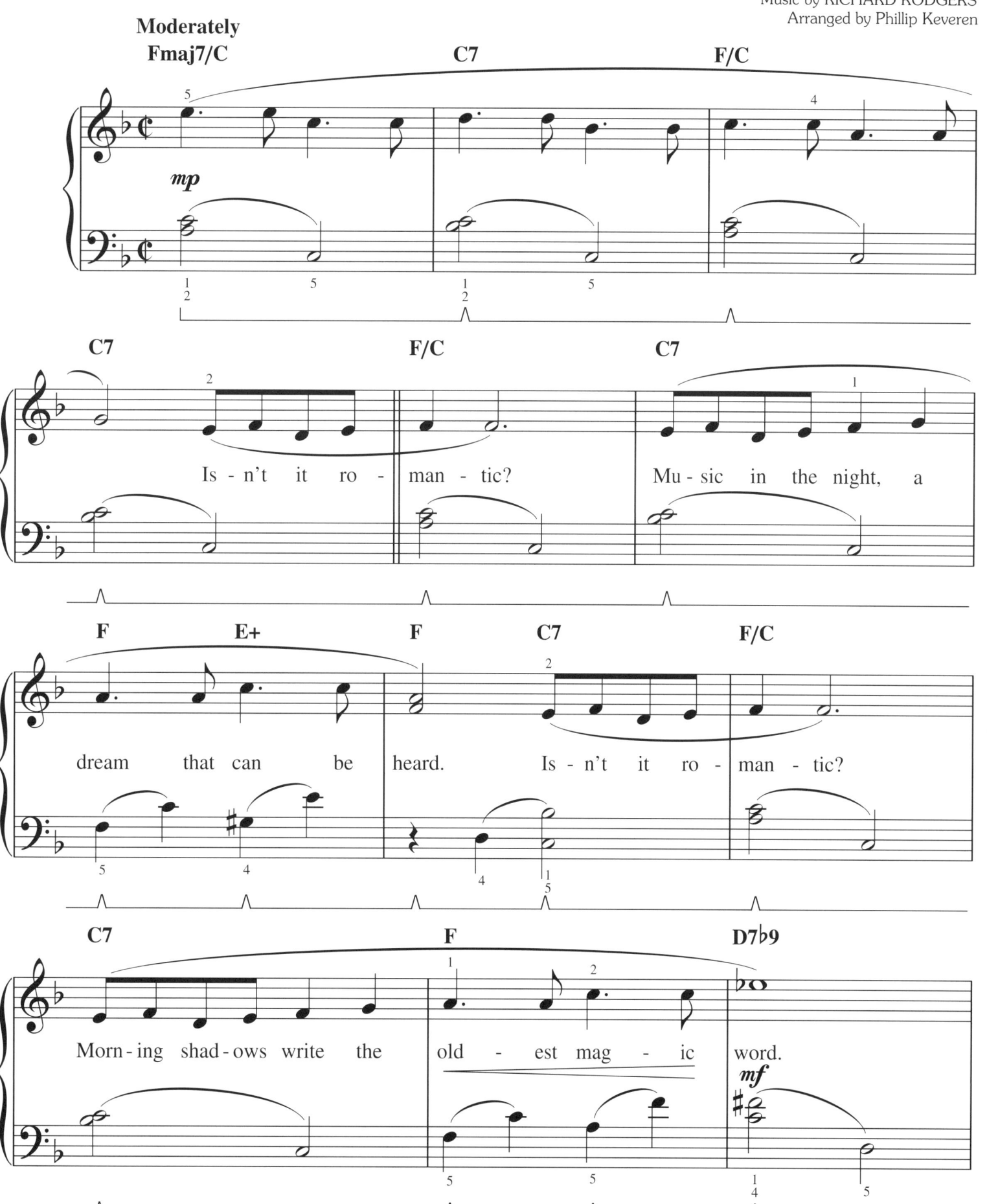

LITTLE GIRL BLUE
from JUMBO

Words by LORENZ HART
Music by RICHARD RODGERS
Arranged by Phillip Keveren

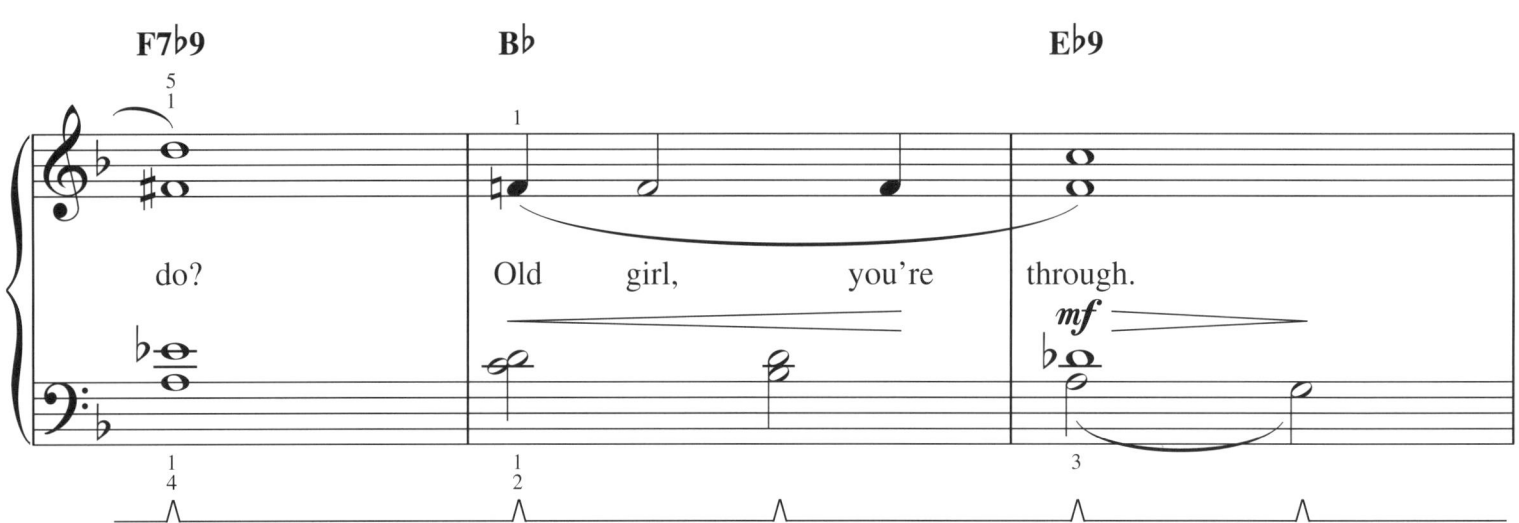
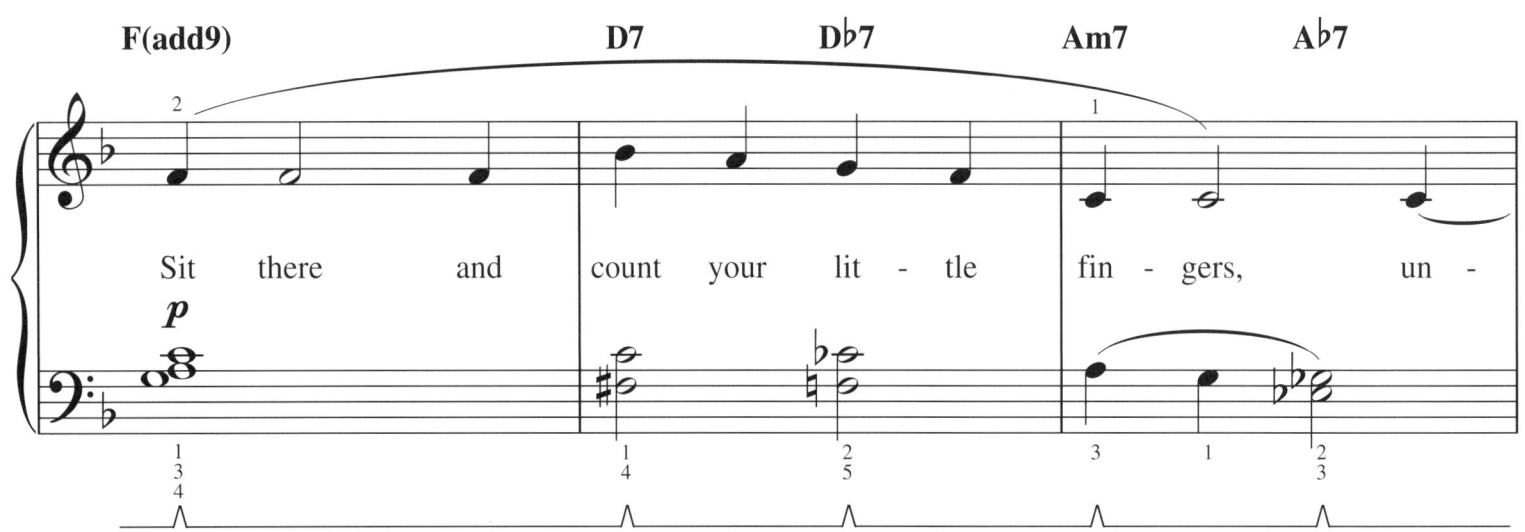

Copyright © 1935 by Williamson Music and Lorenz Hart Publishing Co. in the United States
Copyright Renewed
All Rights Administered by Williamson Music
International Copyright Secured   All Rights Reserved

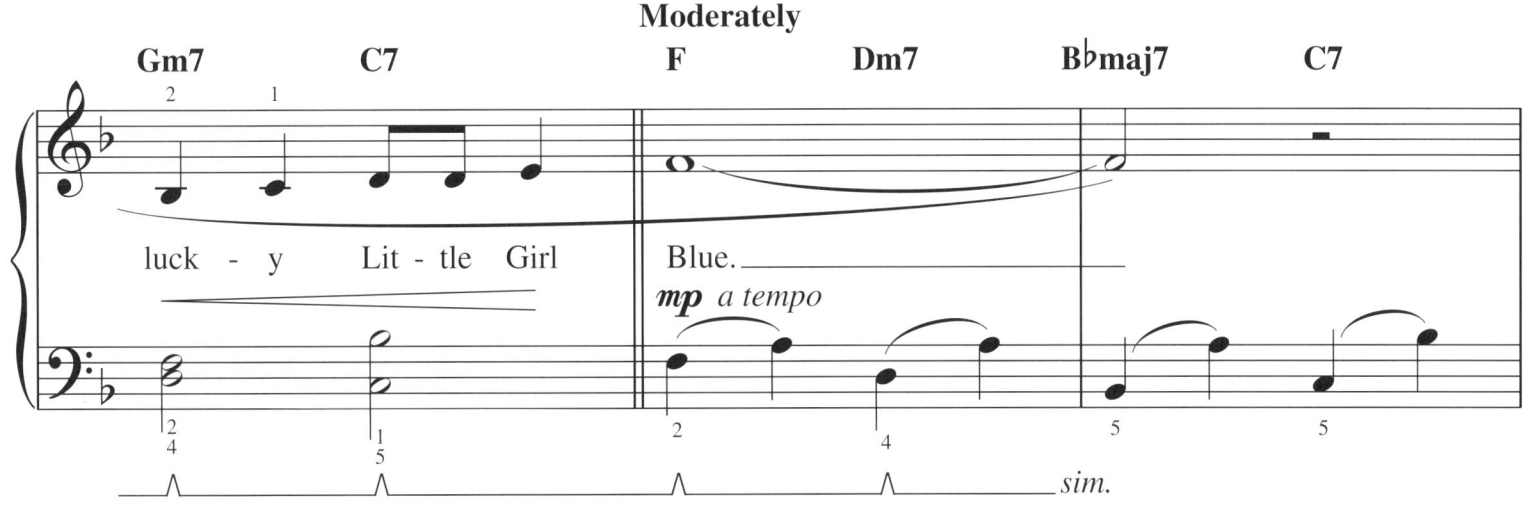
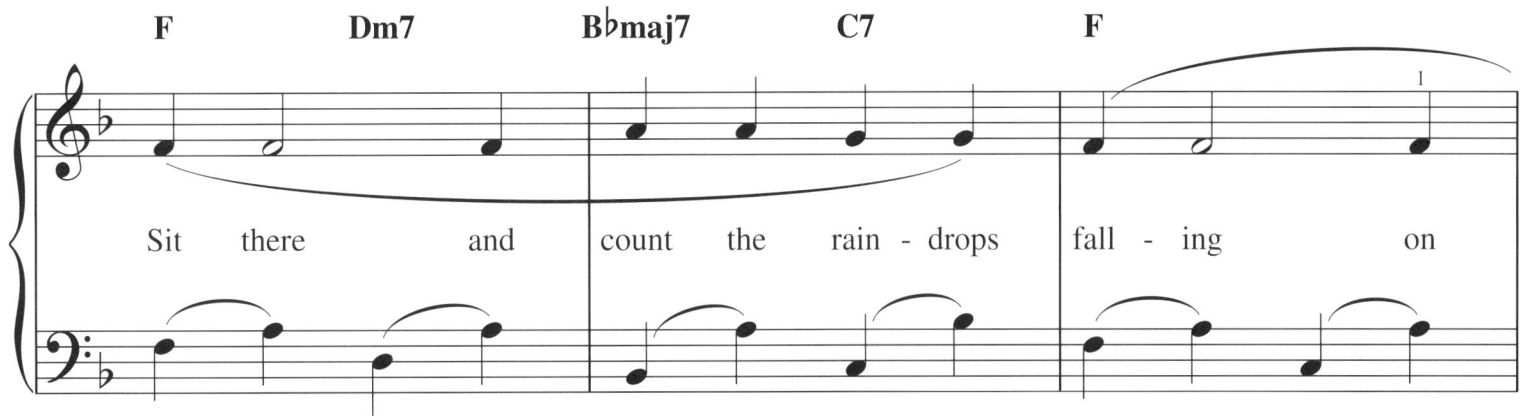

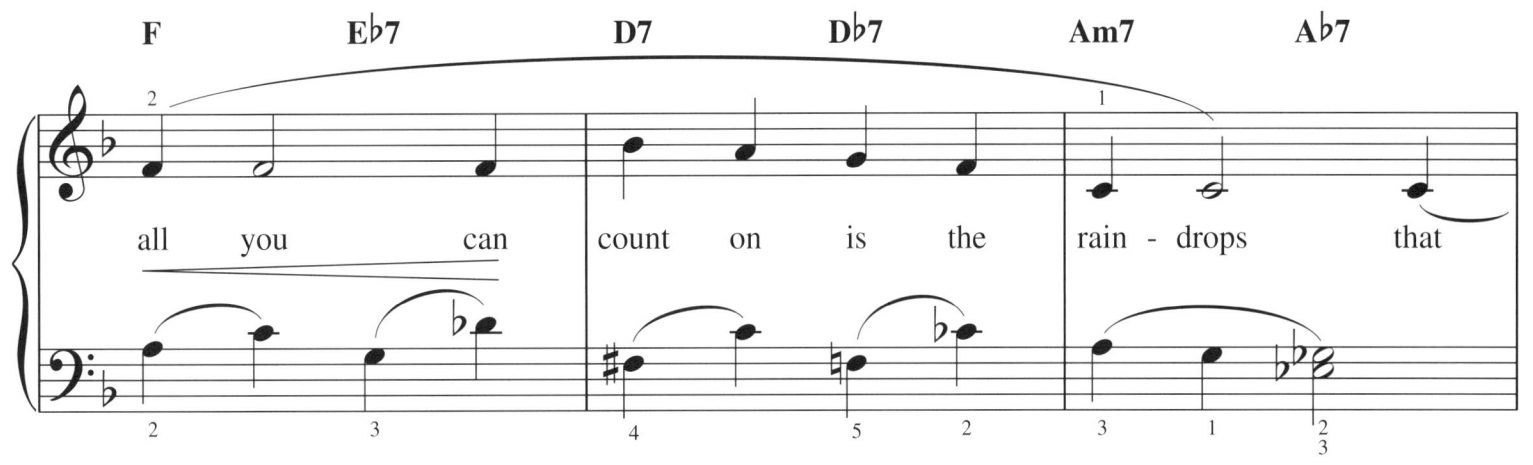

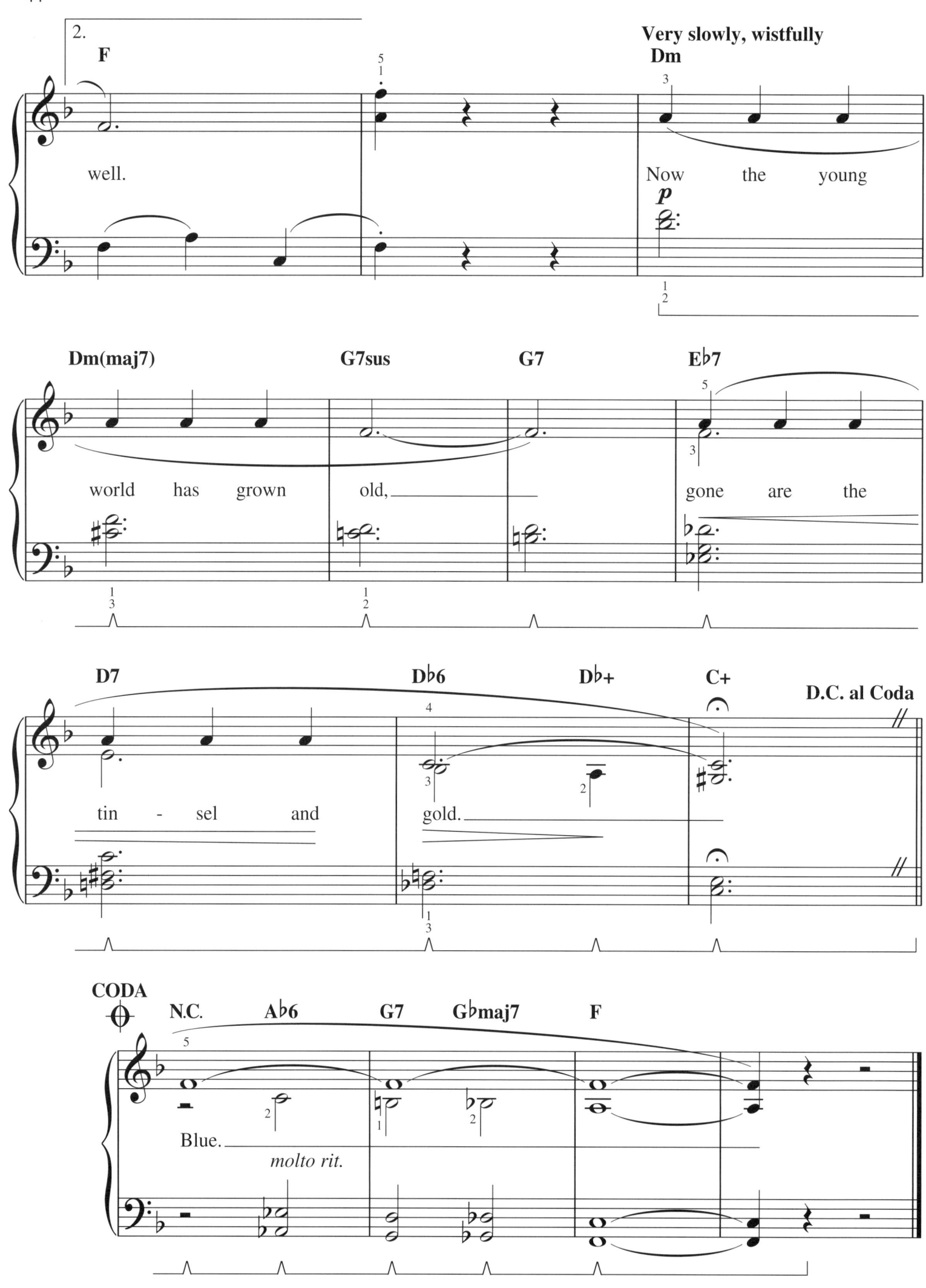

Long Ago
(And Far Away)
from COVER GIRL

Words by IRA GERSHWIN
Music by JEROME KERN
Arranged by Phillip Keveren

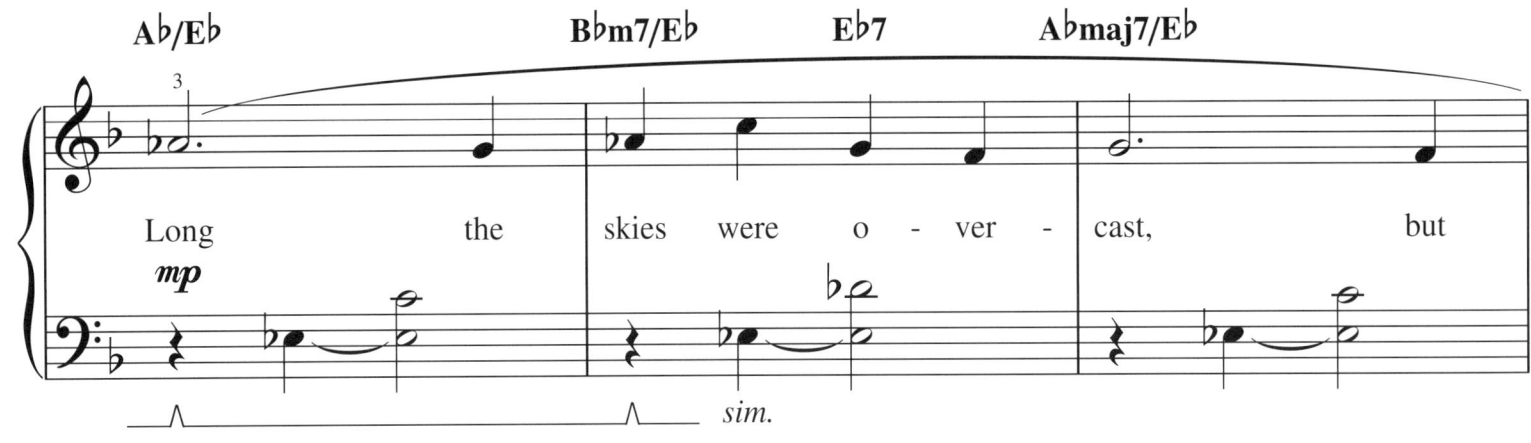
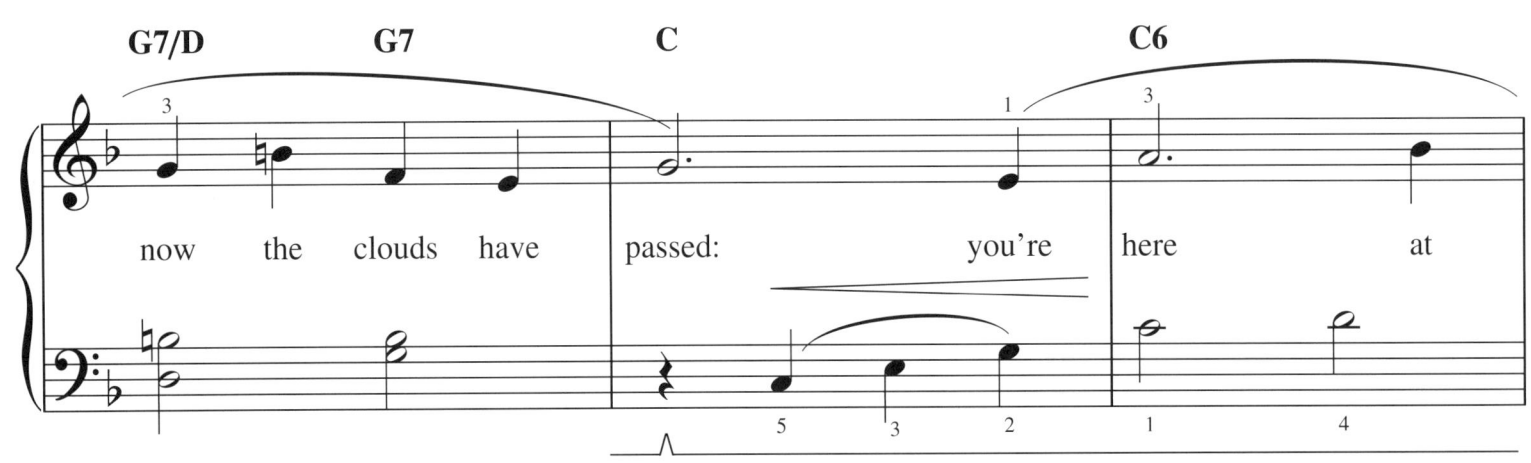
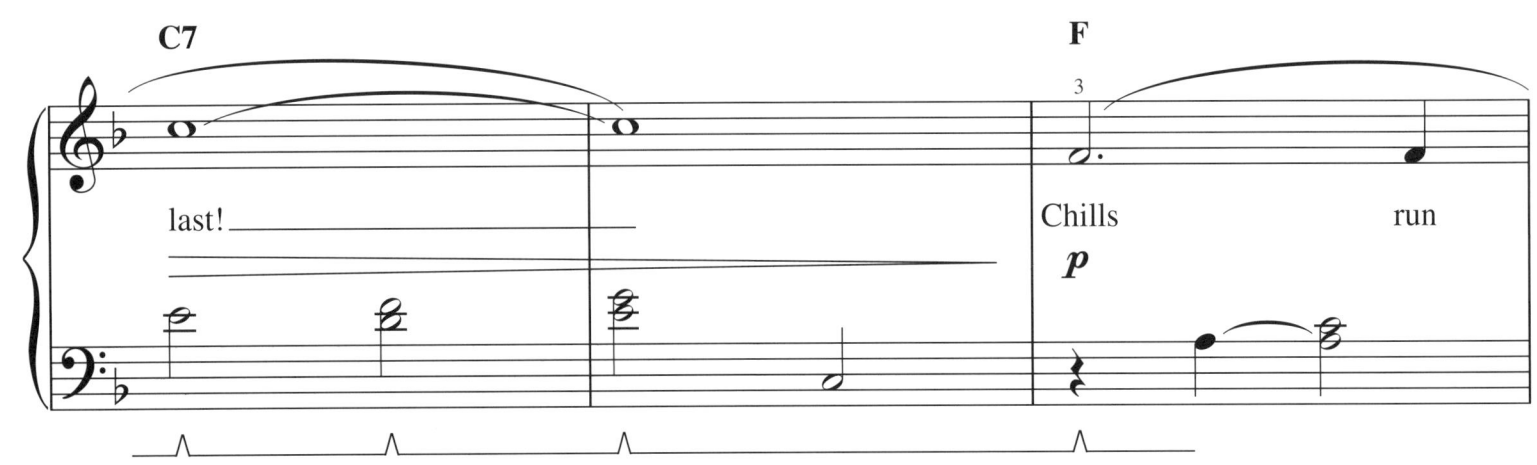
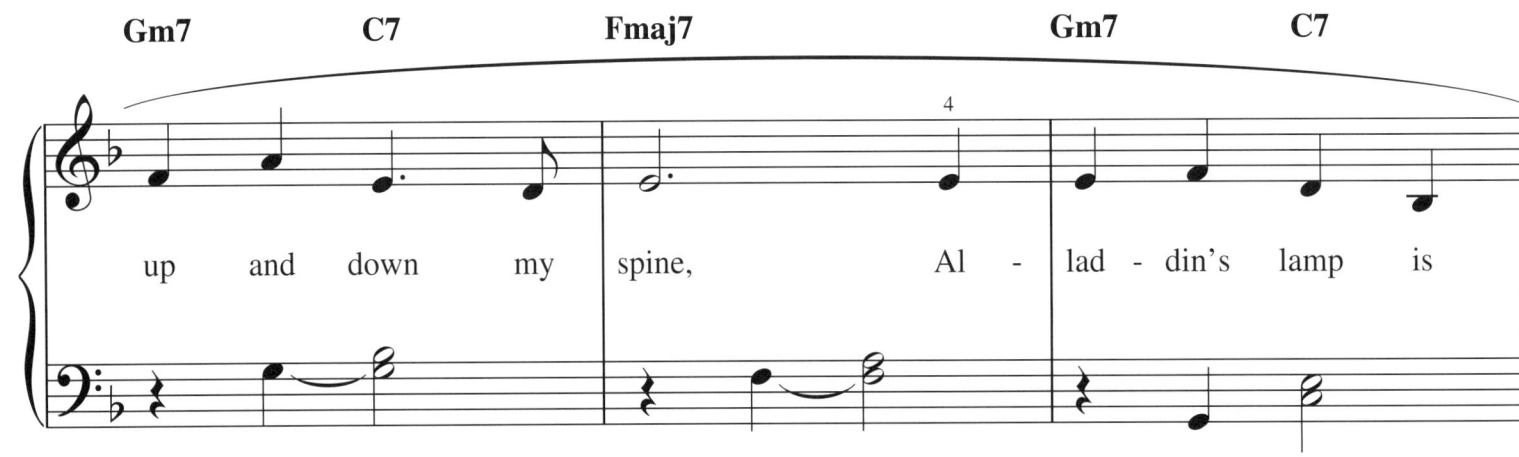

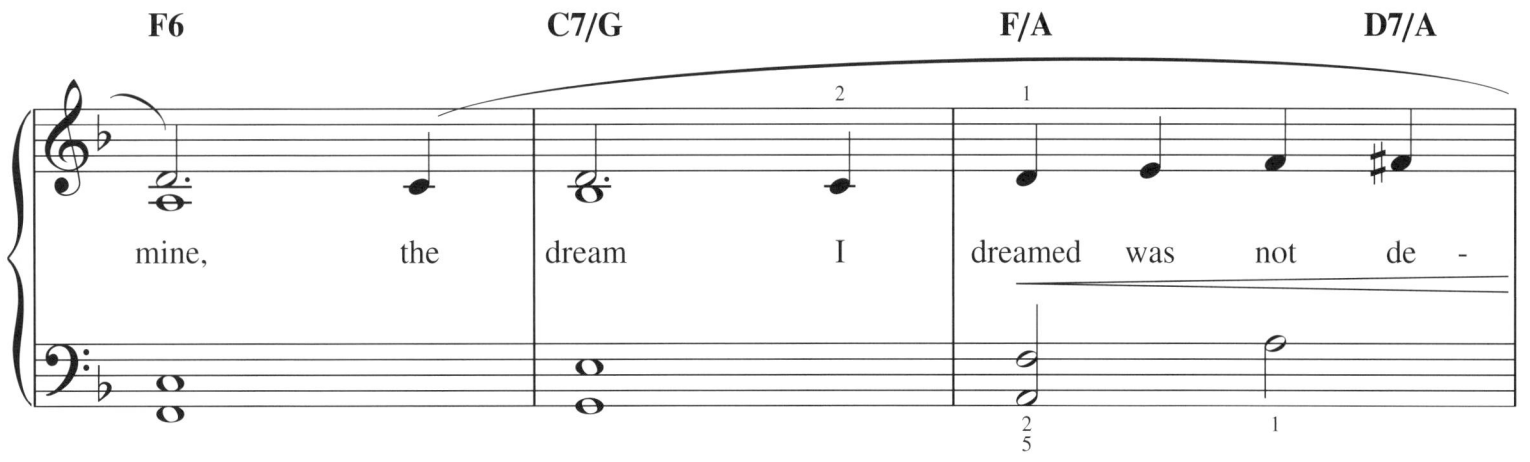
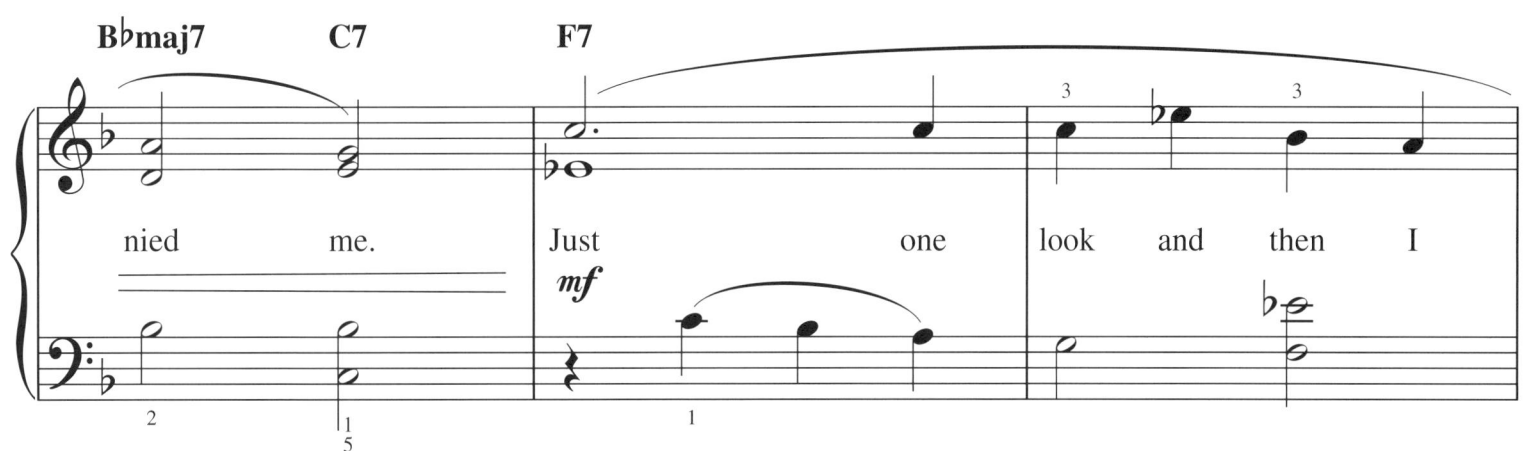
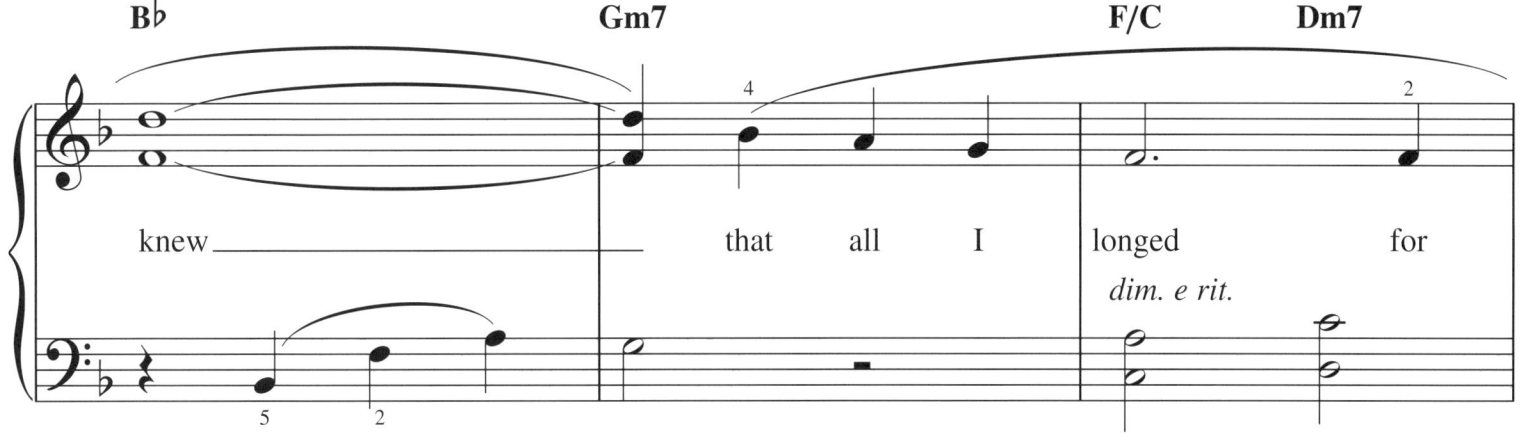
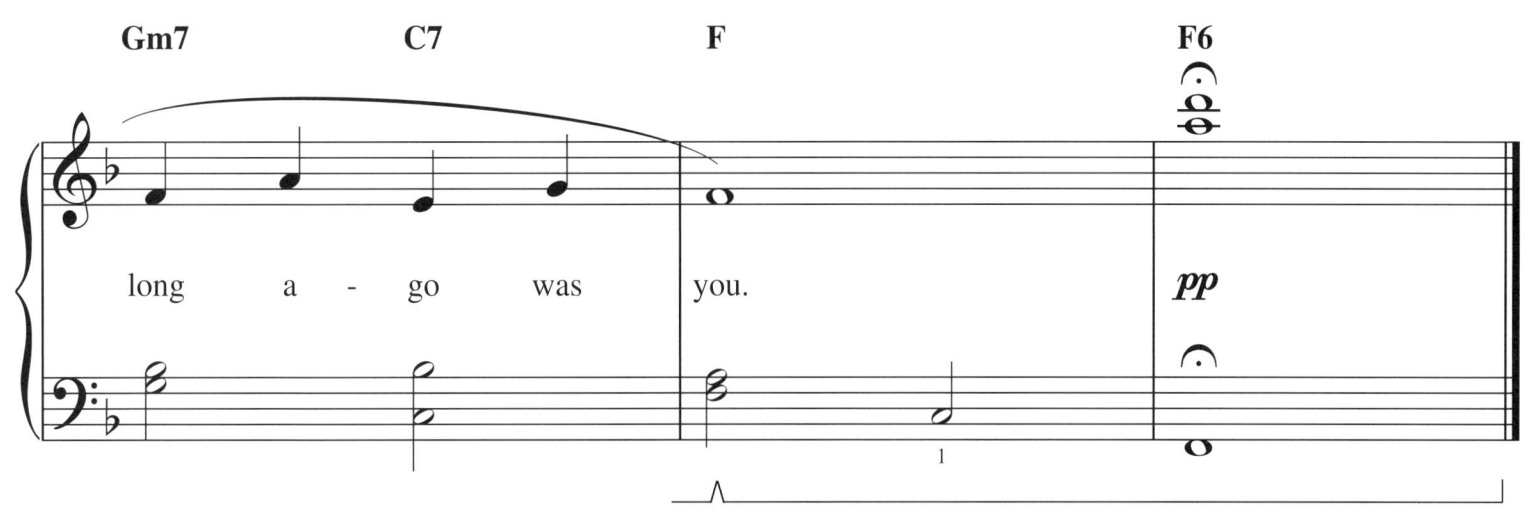

LOVE LETTERS
Theme from the Paramount Picture LOVE LETTERS

Words by EDWARD HEYMAN
Music by VICTOR YOUNG
Arranged by Phillip Keveren

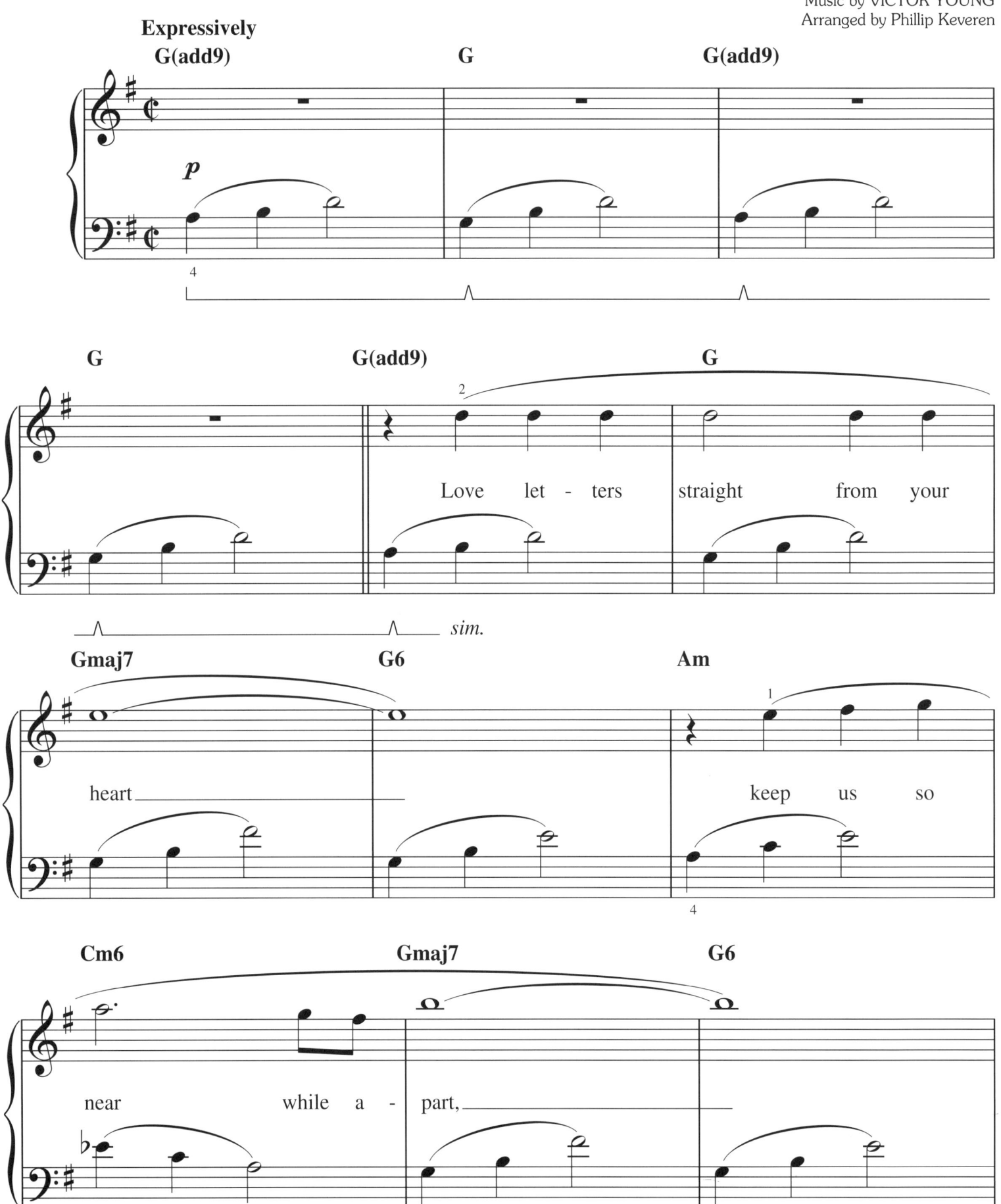

Copyright © 1945 (Renewed 1972) by Famous Music LLC
International Copyright Secured   All Rights Reserved

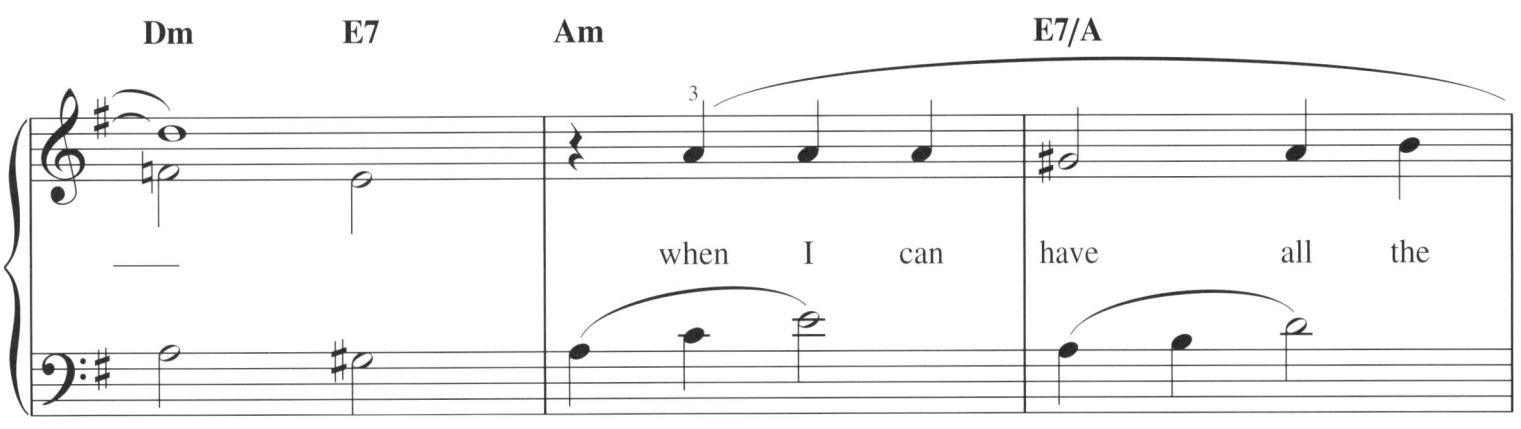
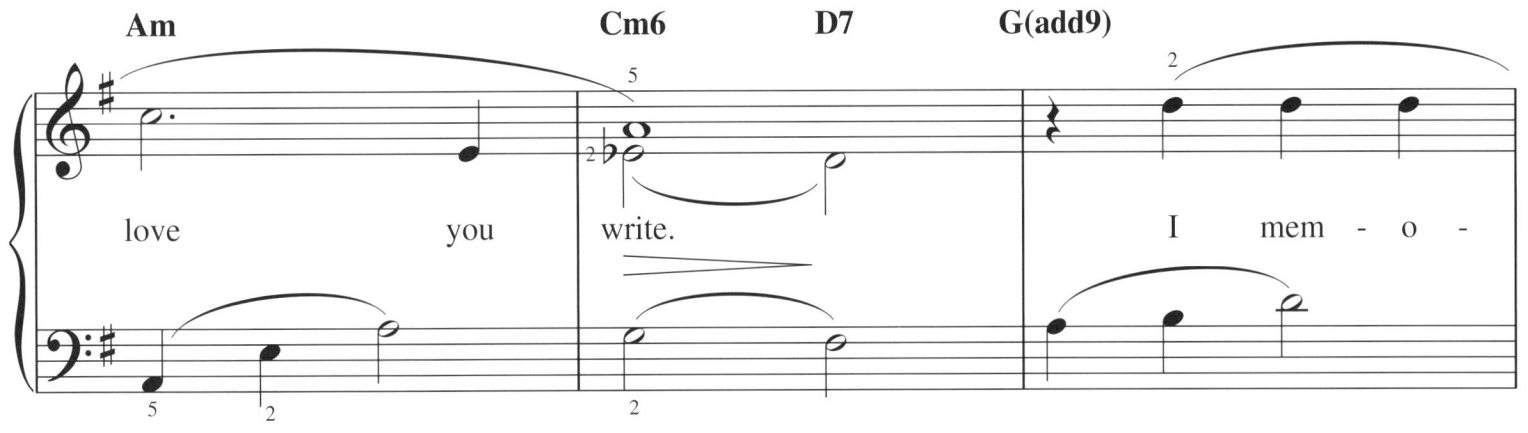
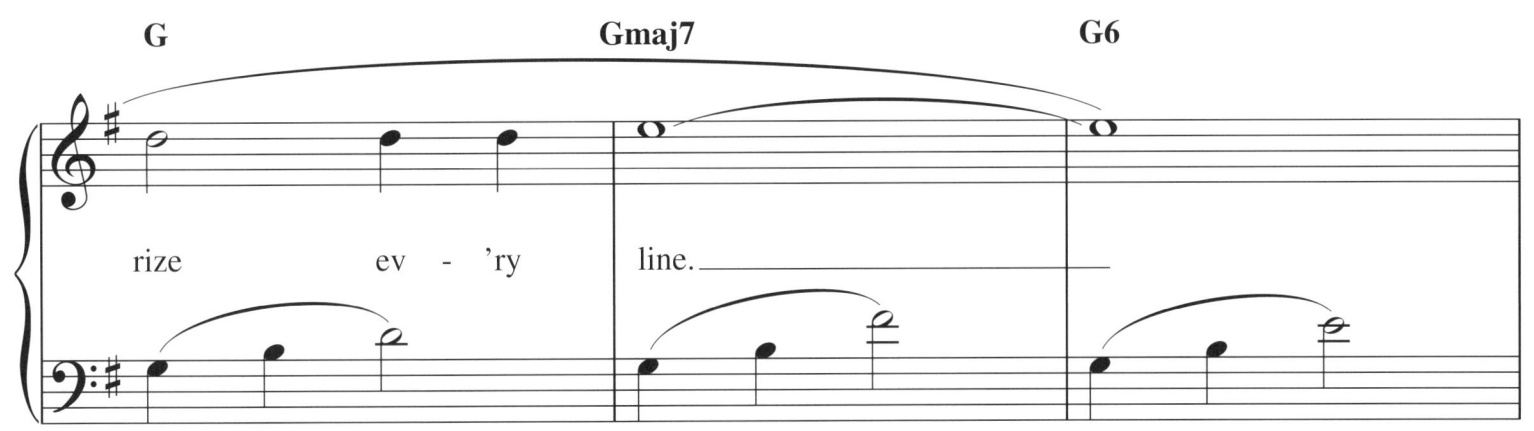

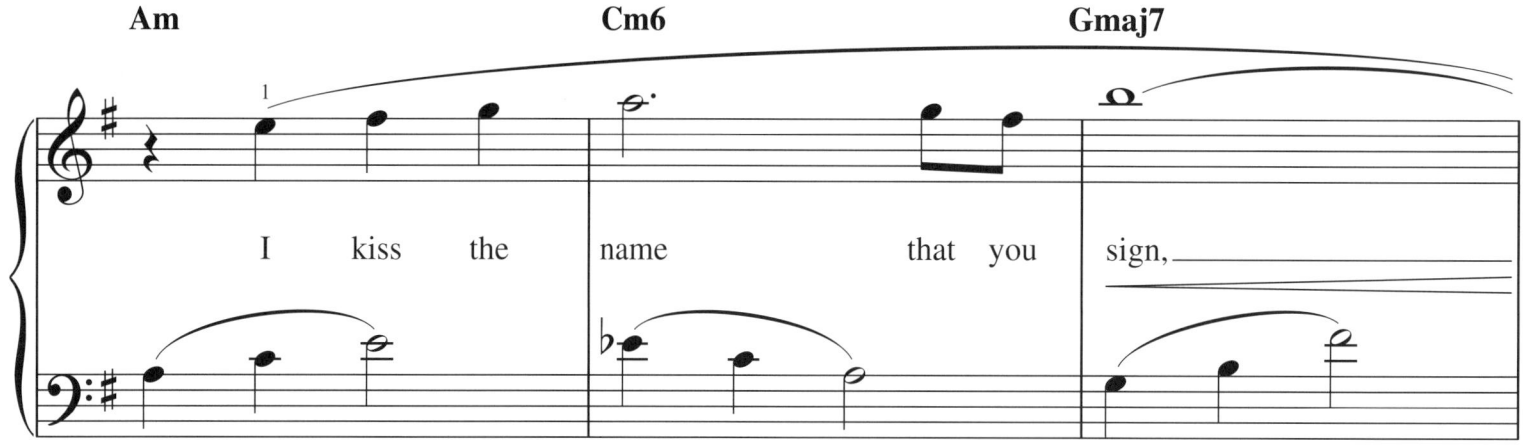
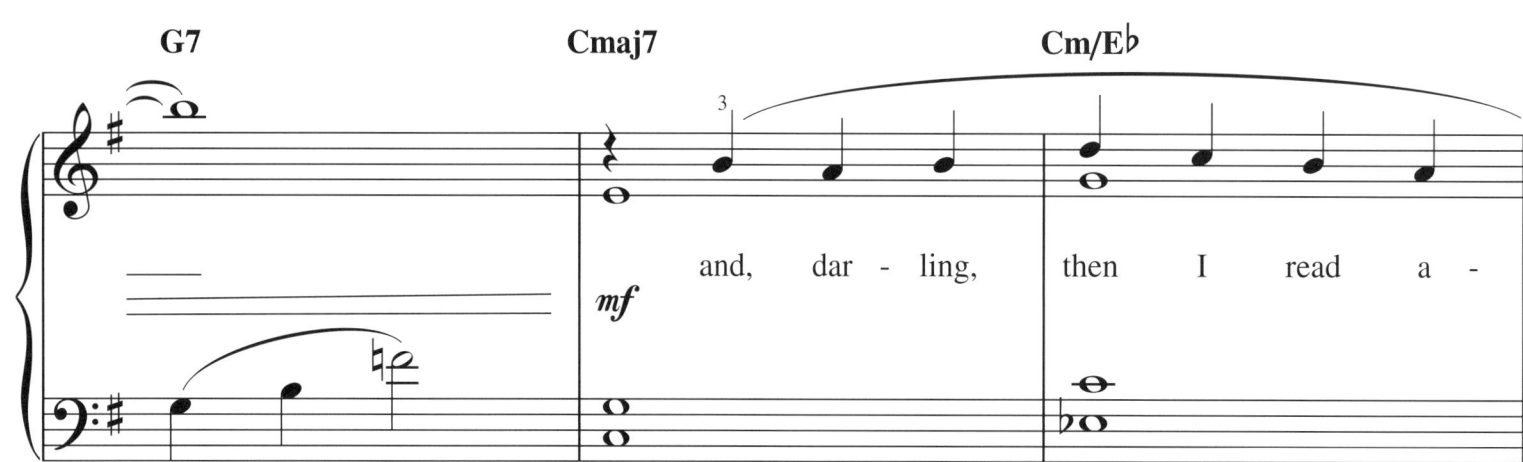
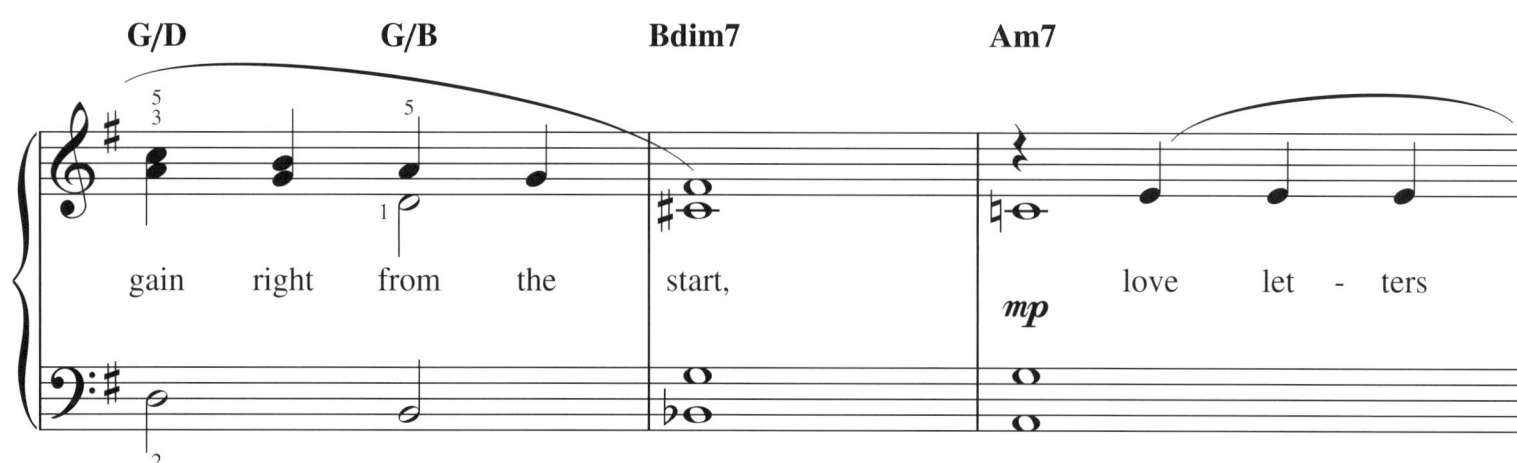
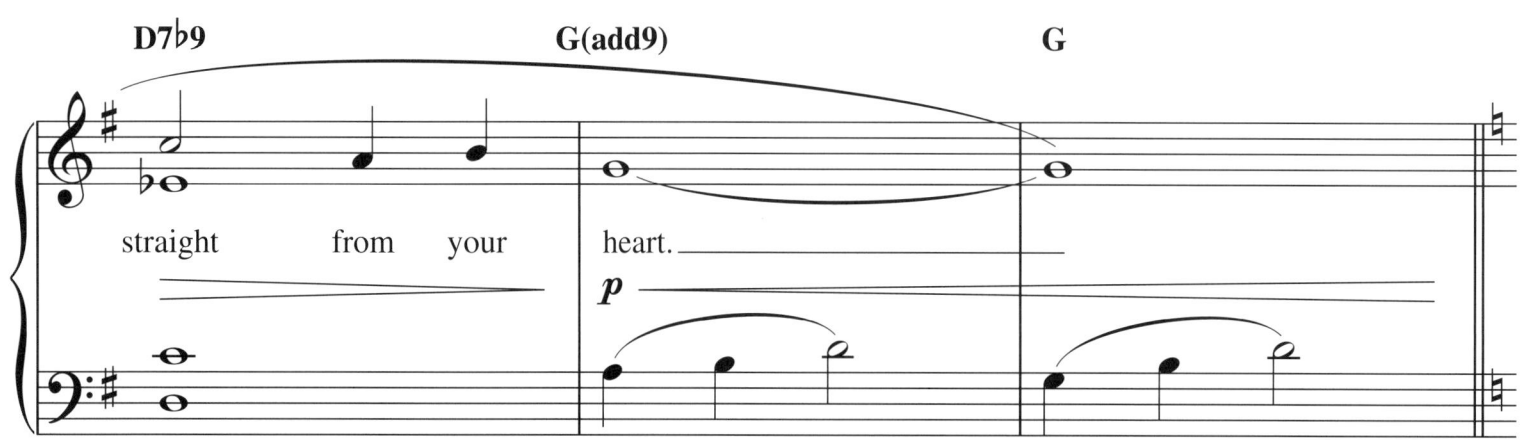

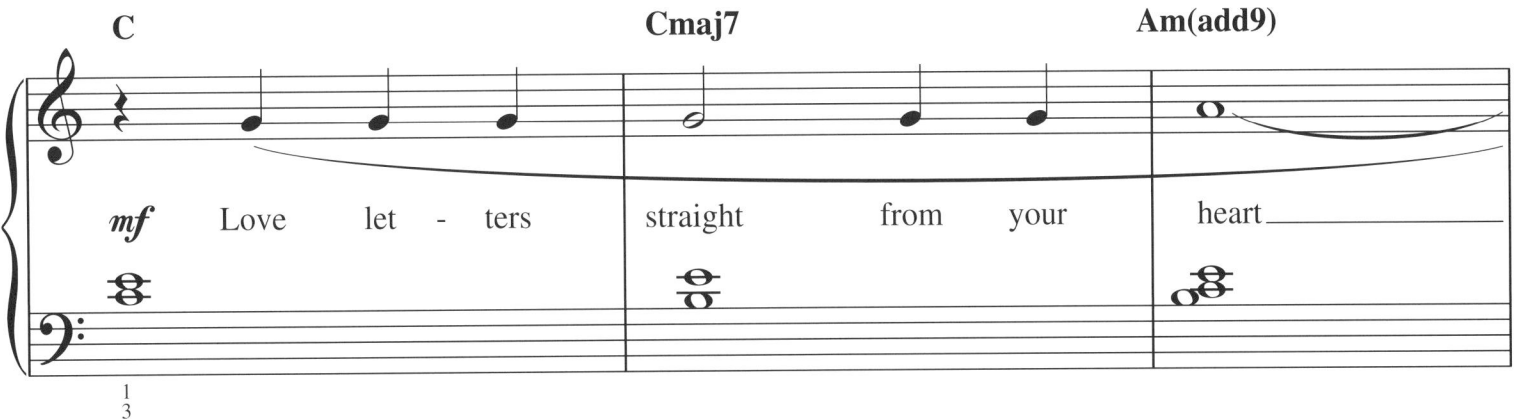

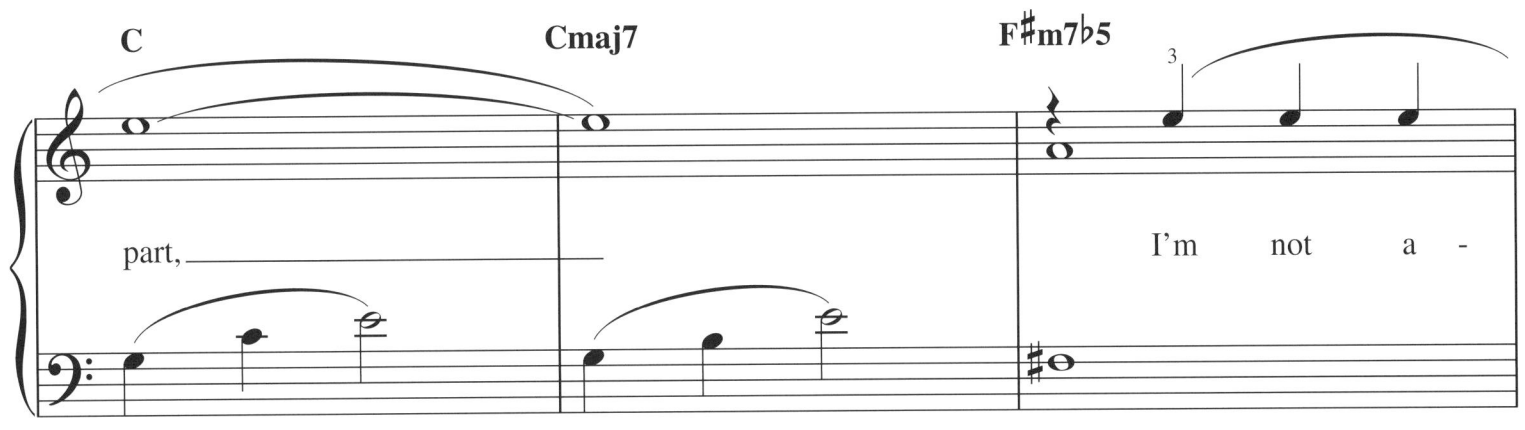
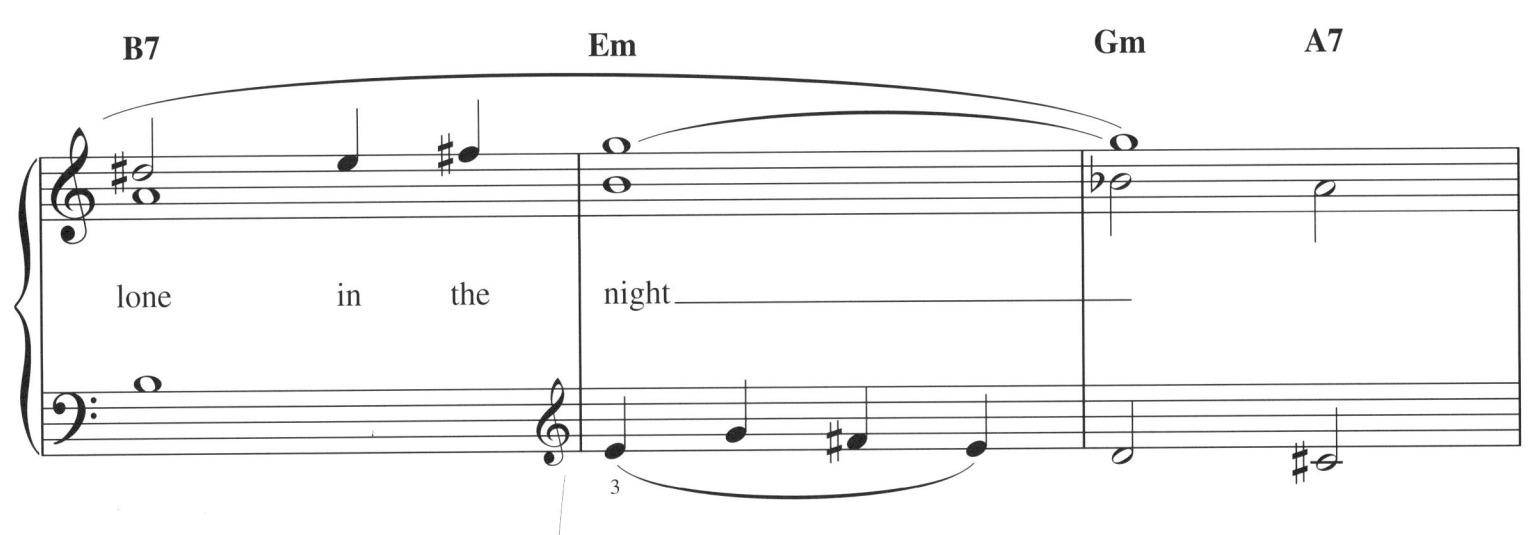

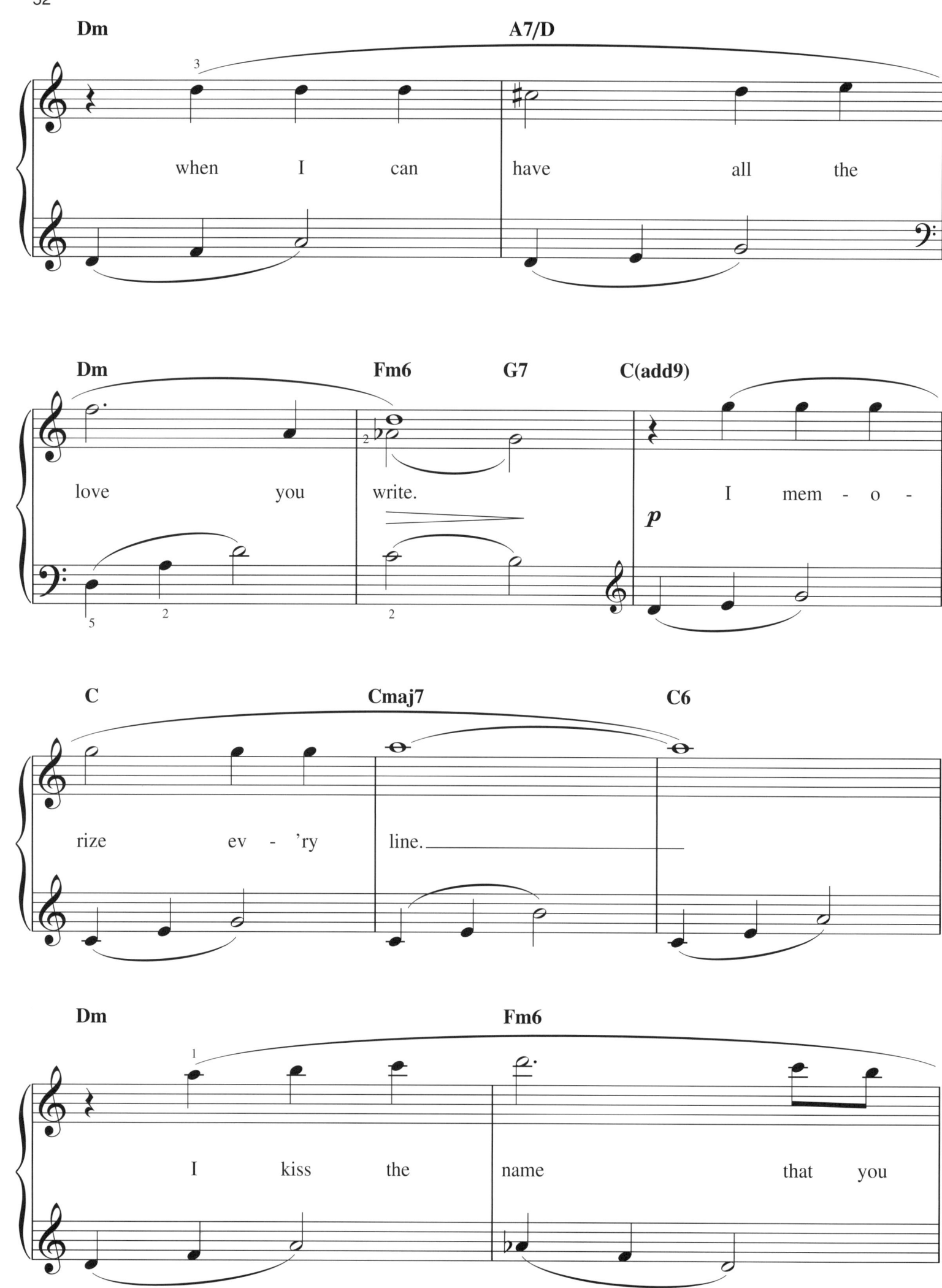

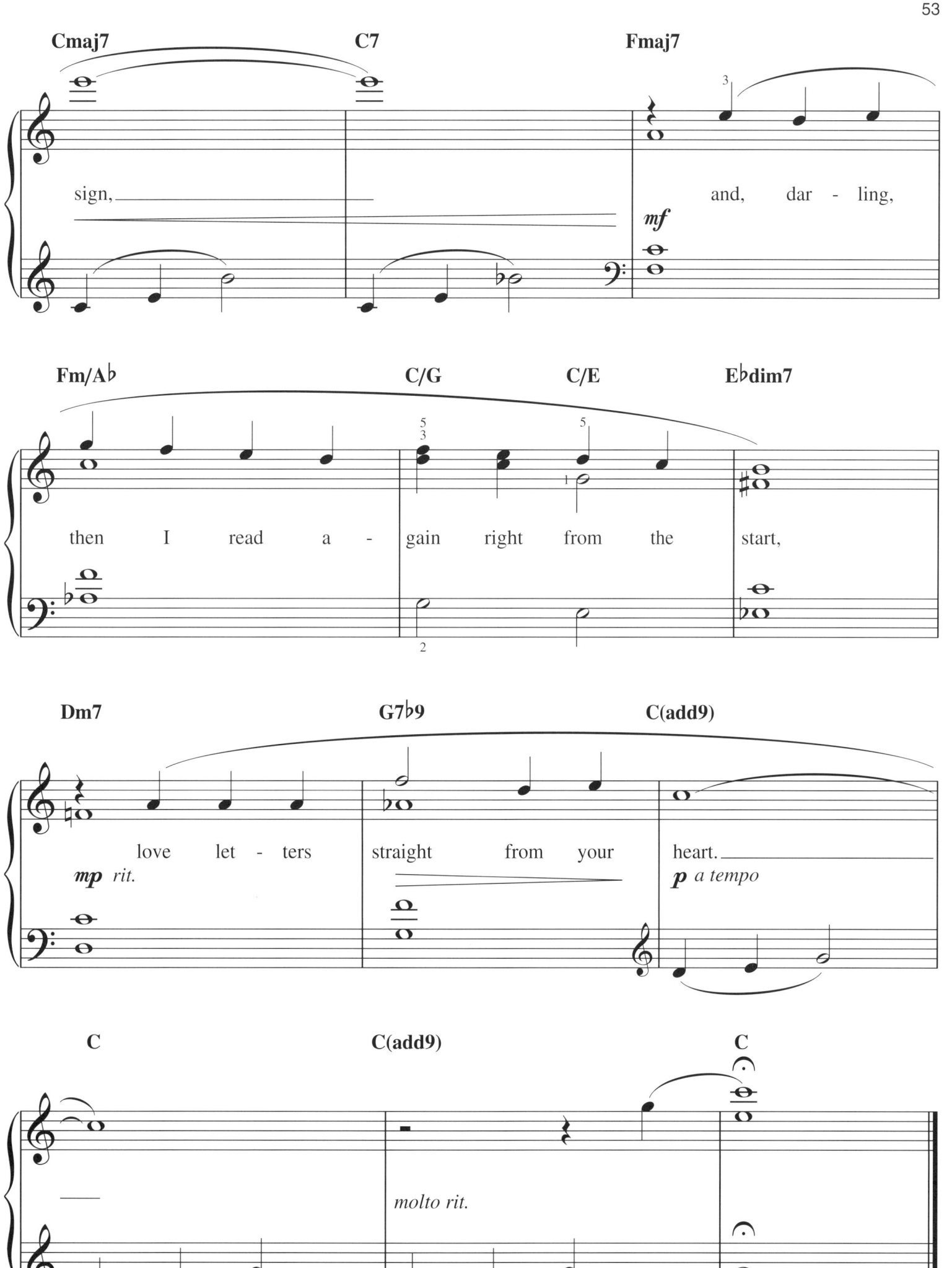

LOVE YOU MADLY

By DUKE ELLINGTON
Arranged by Phillip Keveren

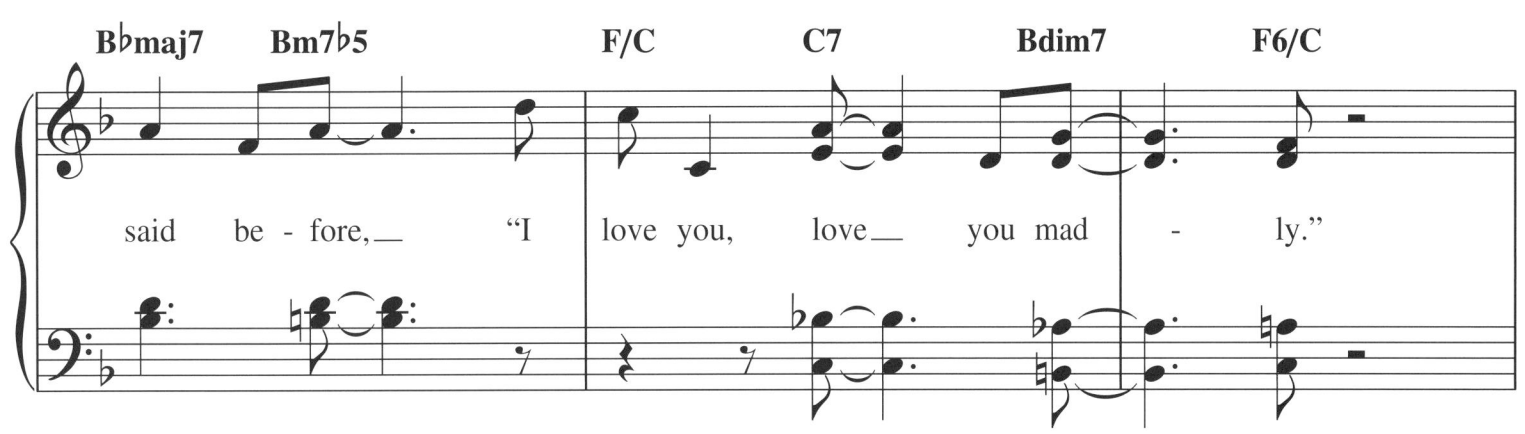
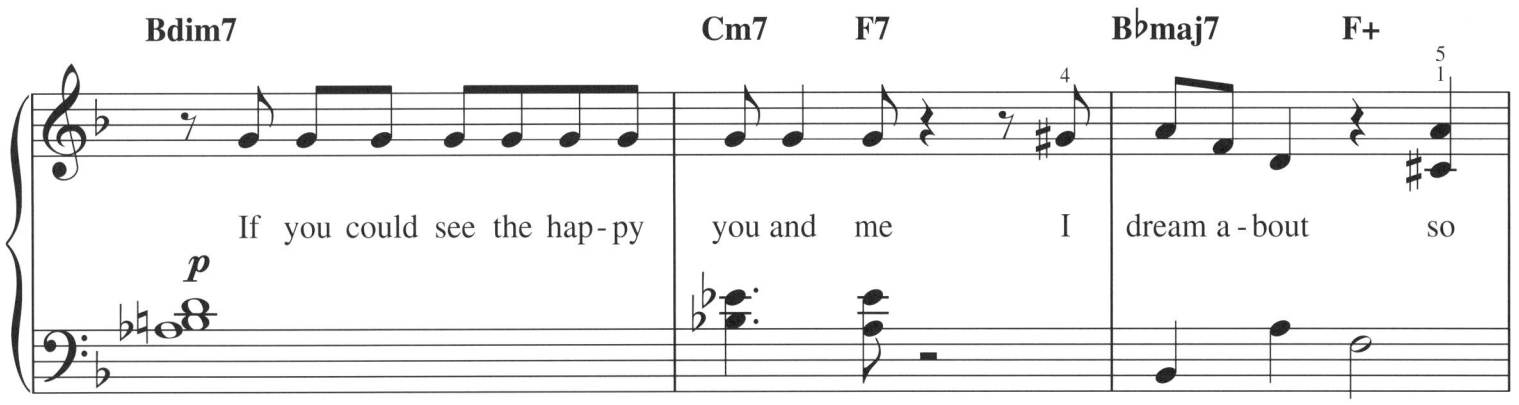
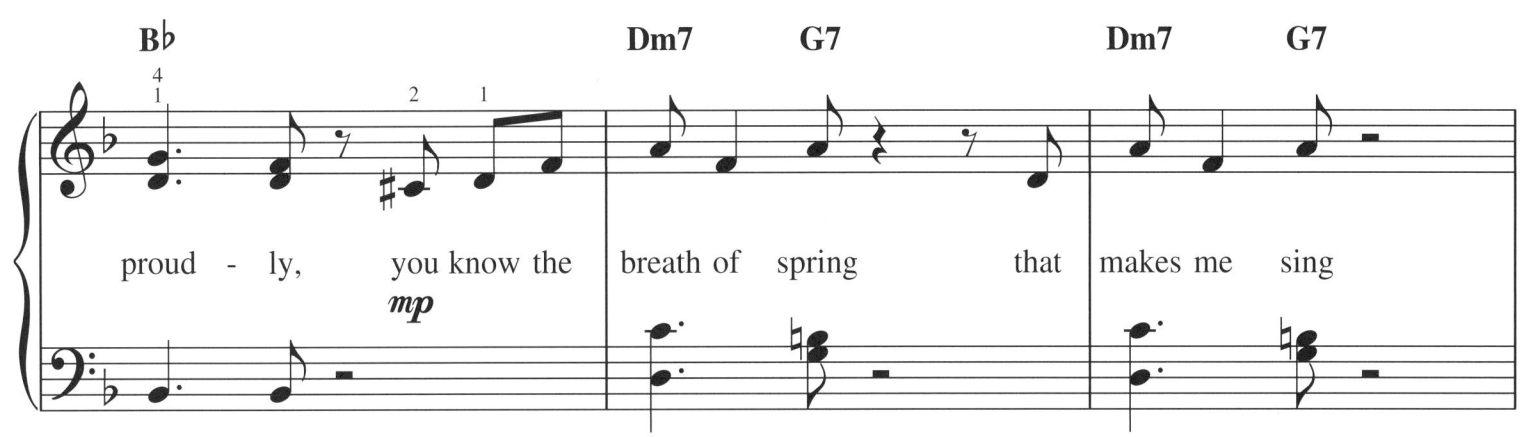

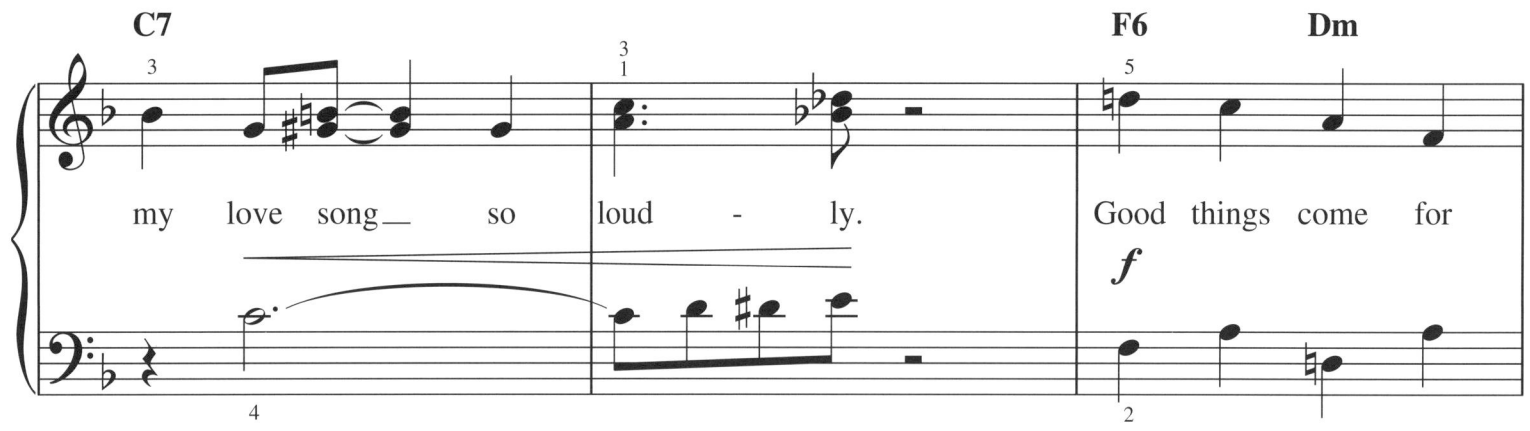

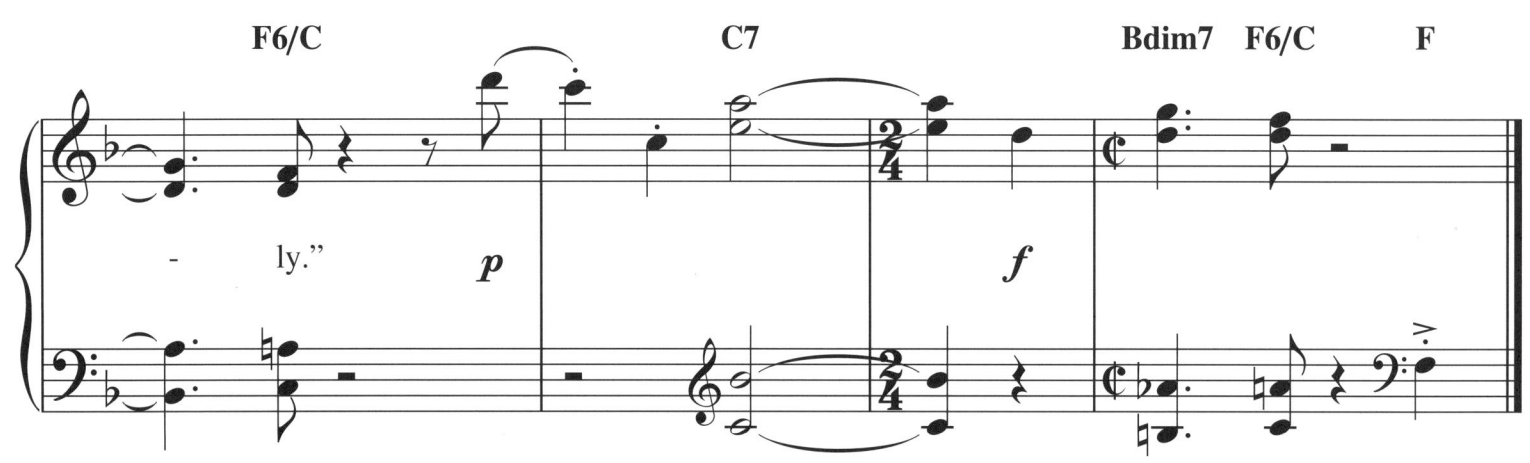

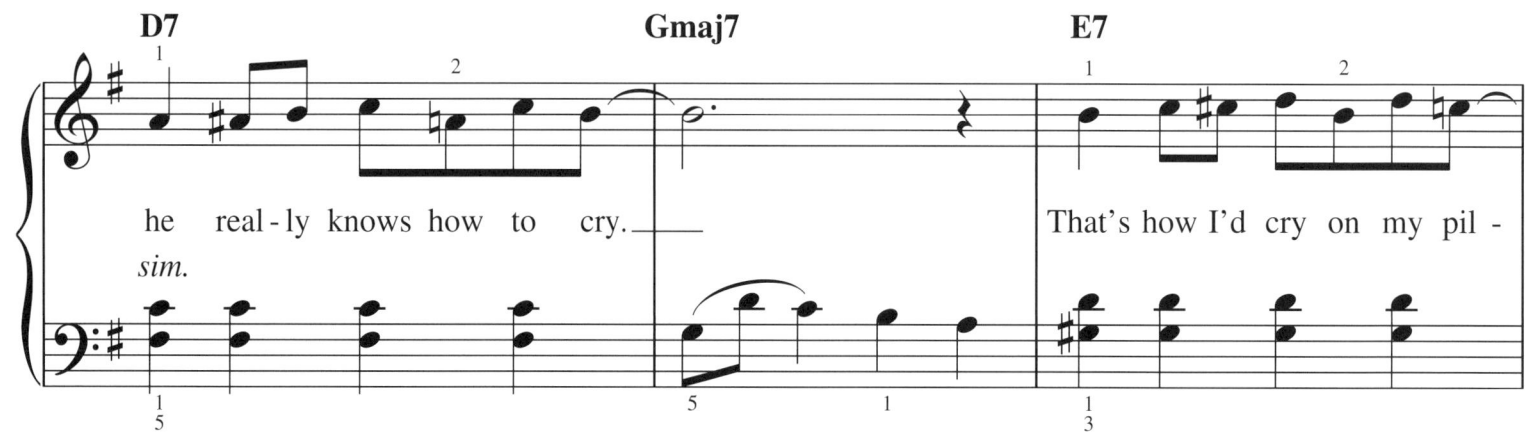
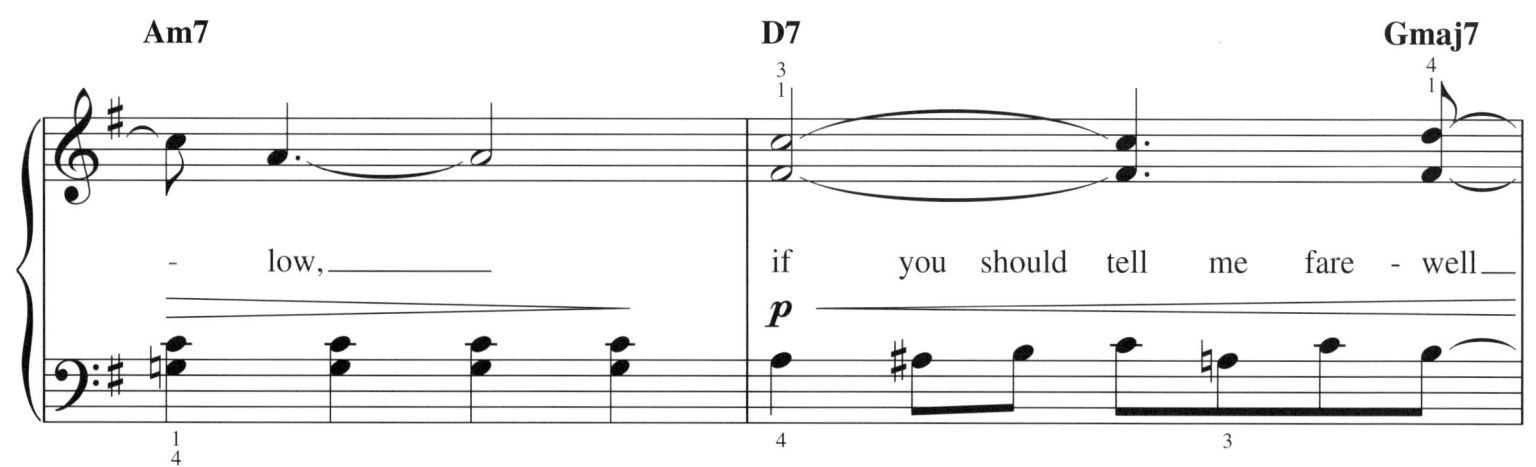

MY FUNNY VALENTINE
from BABES IN ARMS

Words by LORENZ HART
Music by RICHARD RODGERS
Arranged by Phillip Keveren

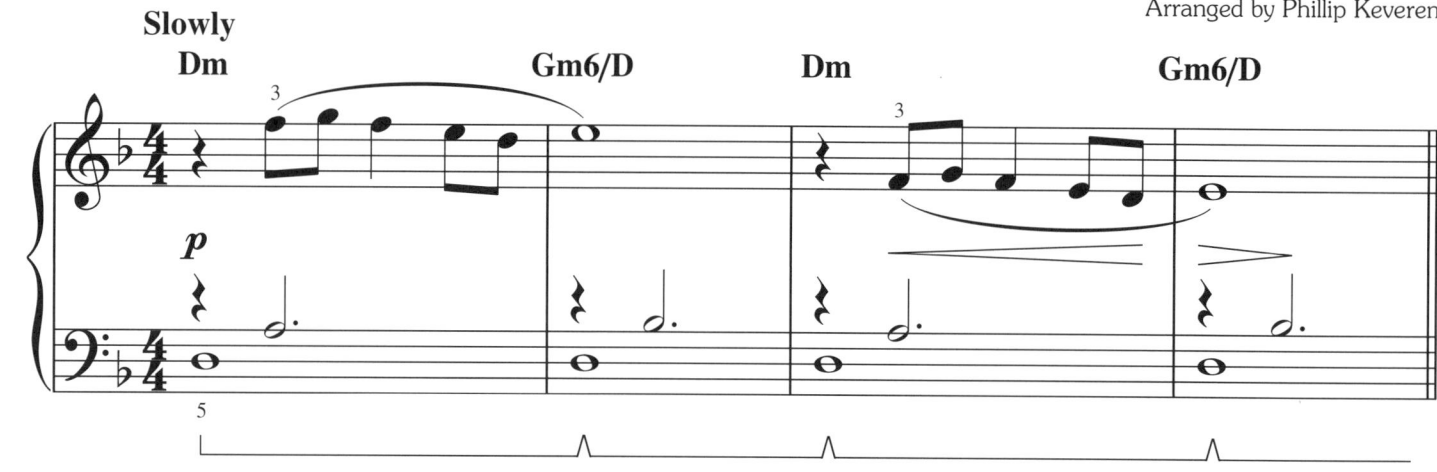
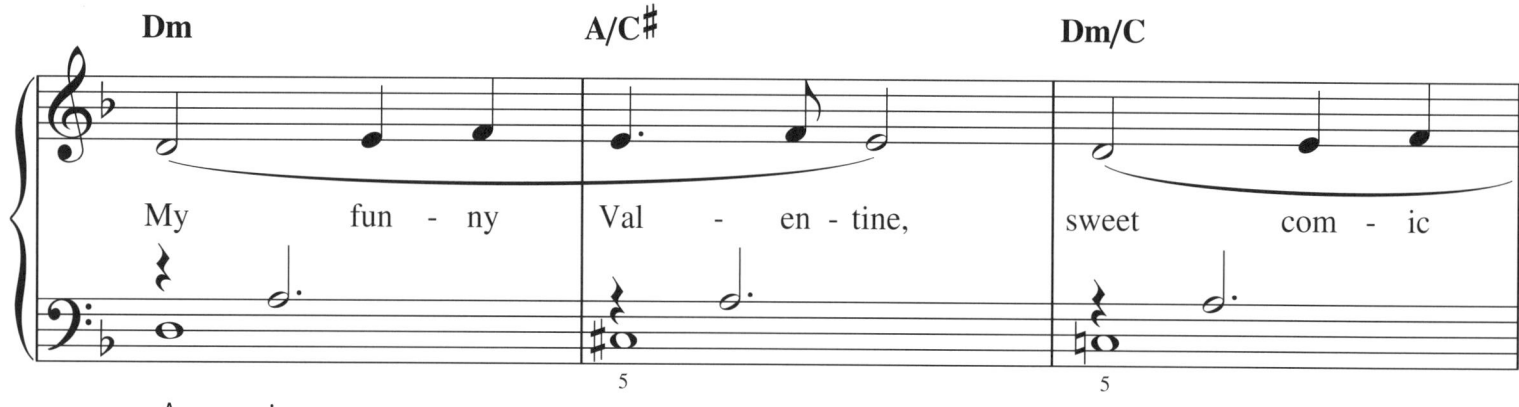
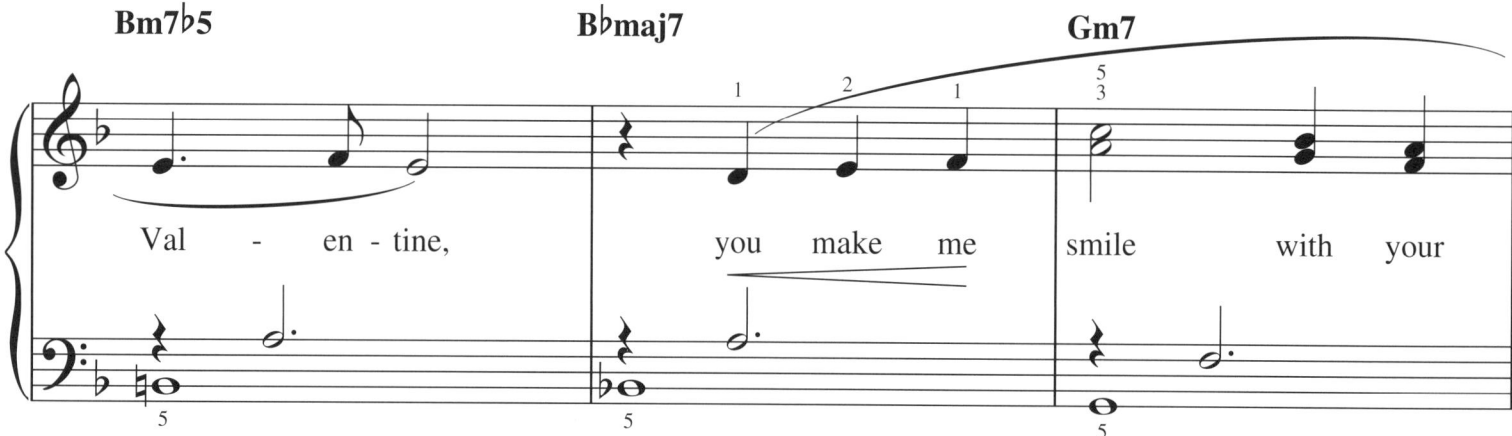

Copyright © 1937 (Renewed) by Chappell & Co.
Rights for the Extended Renewal Term in the U.S. Controlled by Williamson Music and WB Music Corp. o/b/o The Estate Of Lorenz Hart
International Copyright Secured   All Rights Reserved

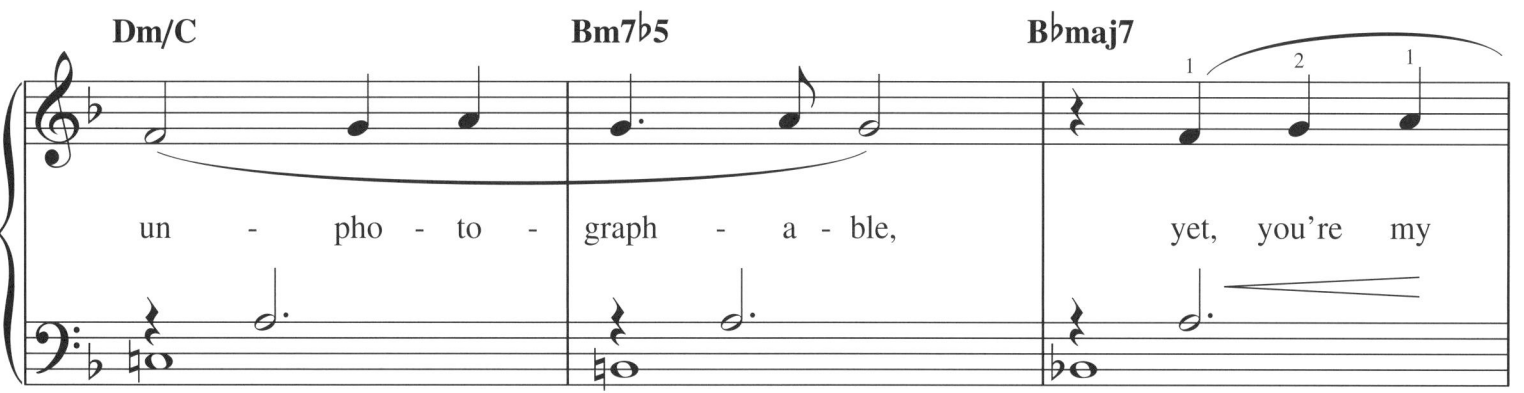
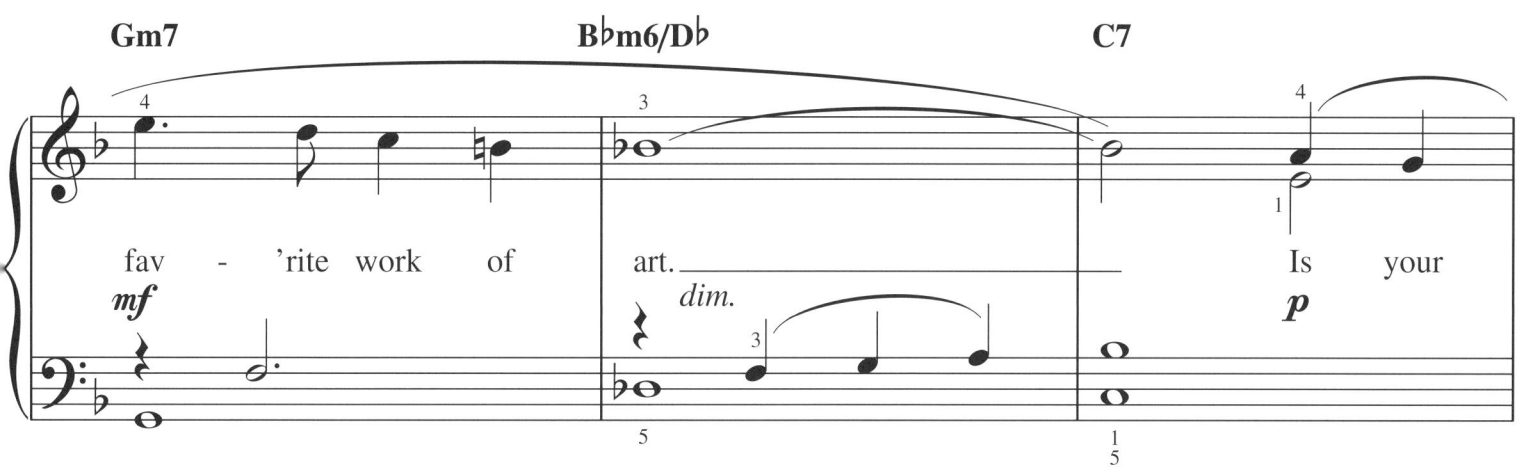

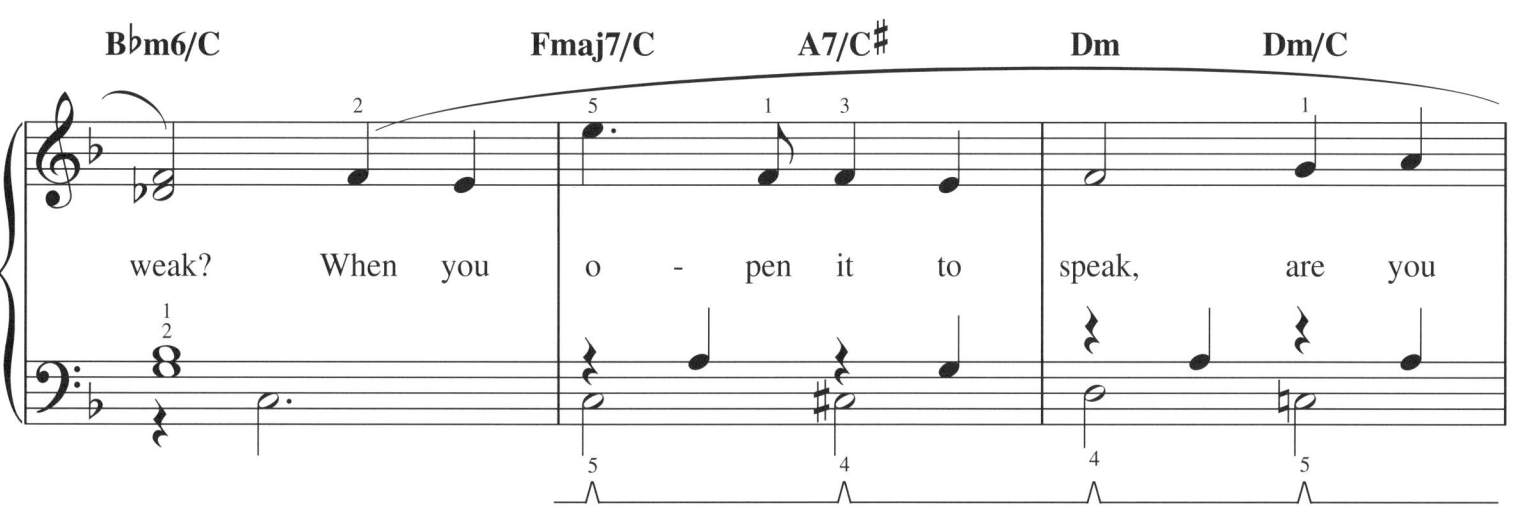

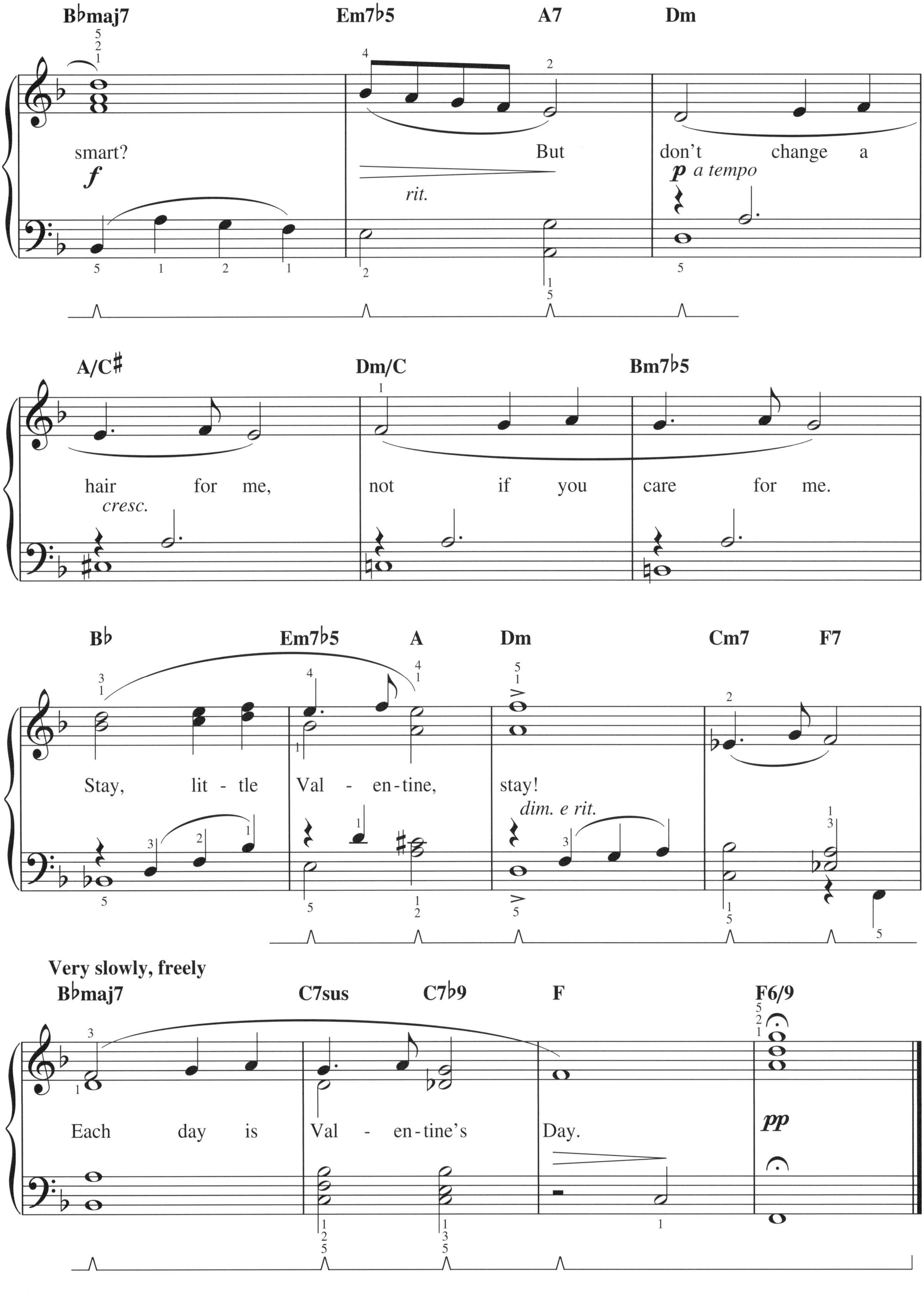
B♭maj7
Em7♭5
A7
Dm
smart?
But
don't change a
f
rit.
p a tempo
A/C♯
Dm/C
Bm7♭5
hair for me,
not if you
care for me.
cresc.
B♭
Em7♭5
A
Dm
Cm7
F7
Stay, lit - tle
Val - en - tine,
stay!
dim. e rit.
Very slowly, freely
B♭maj7
C7sus
C7♭9
F
F6/9
Each day is
Val - en - tine's
Day.
pp

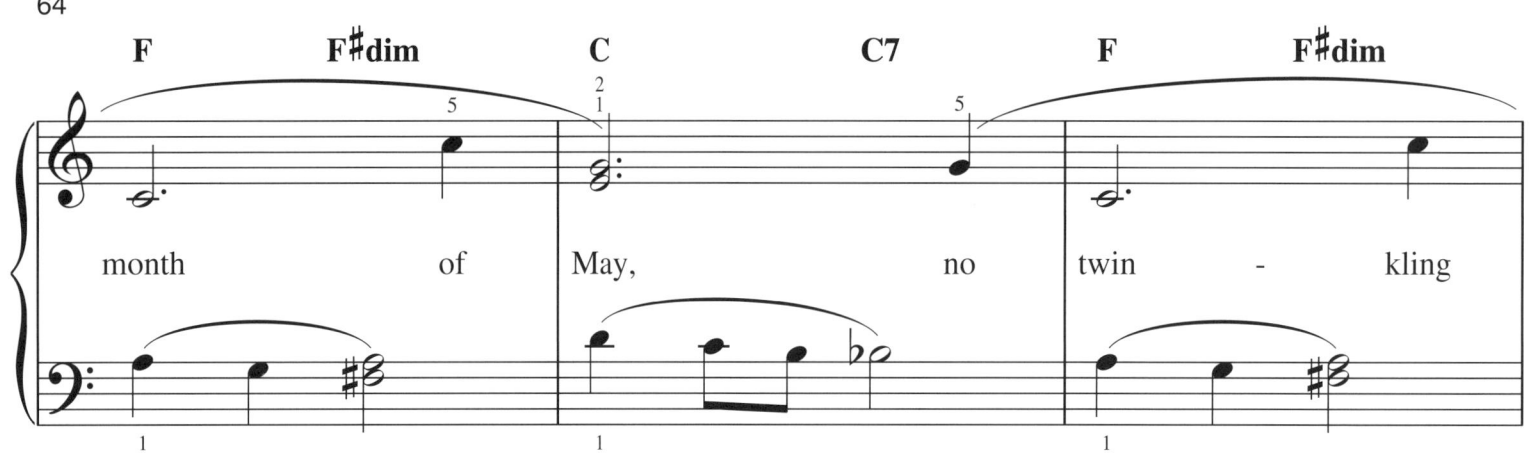
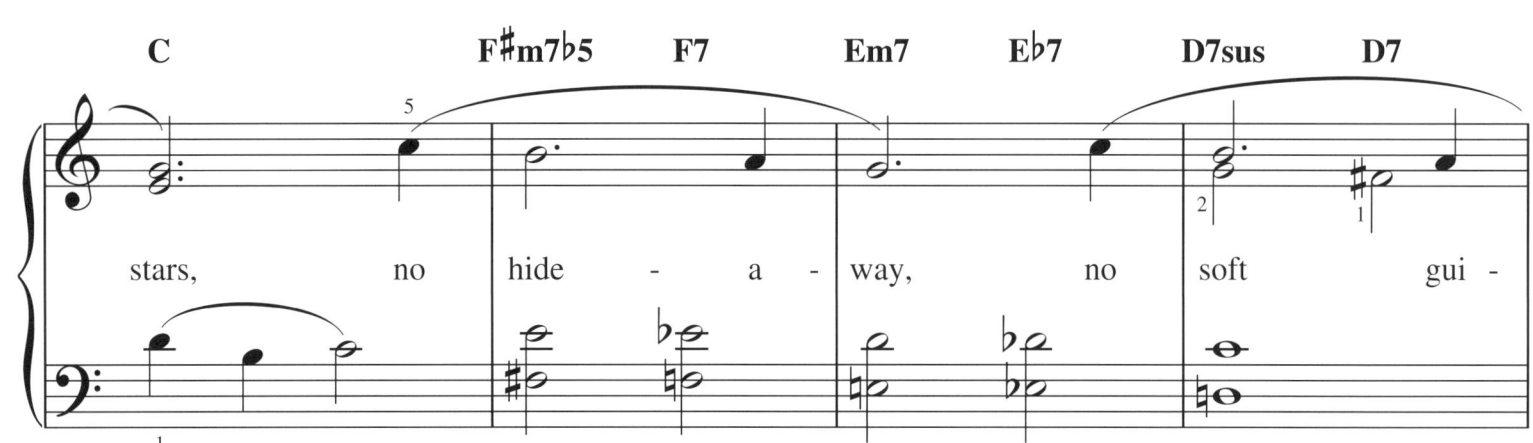
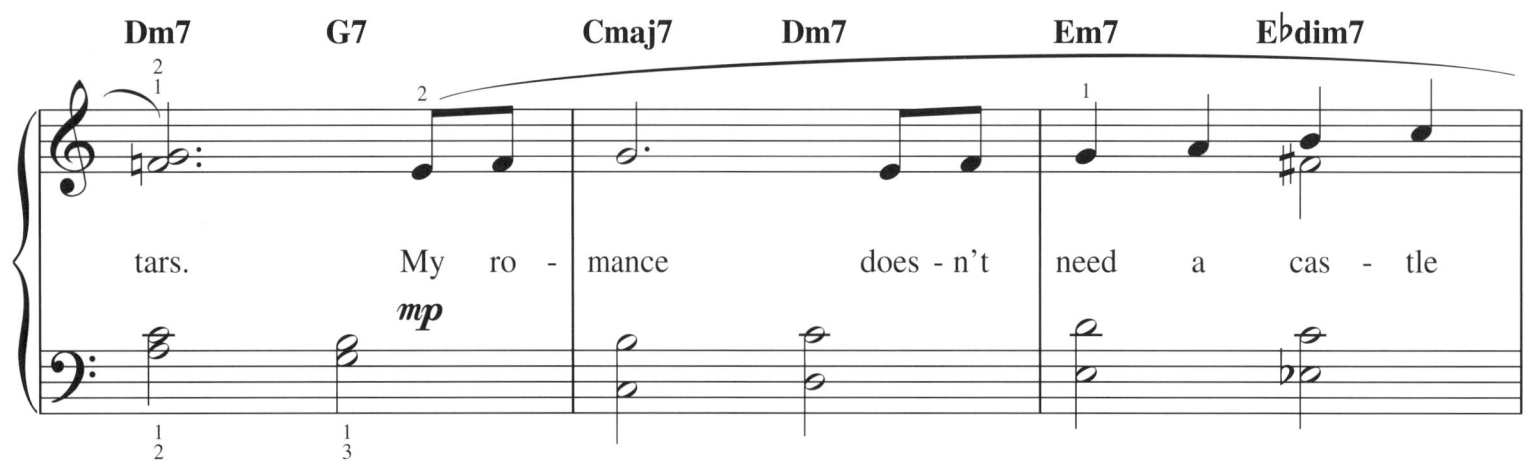
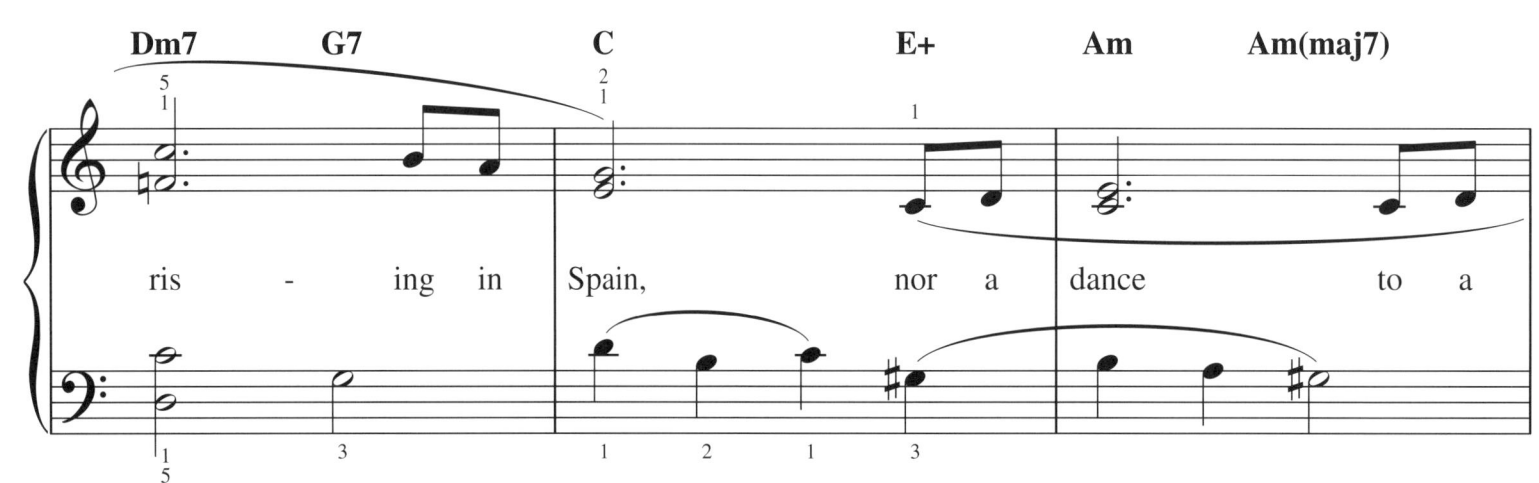

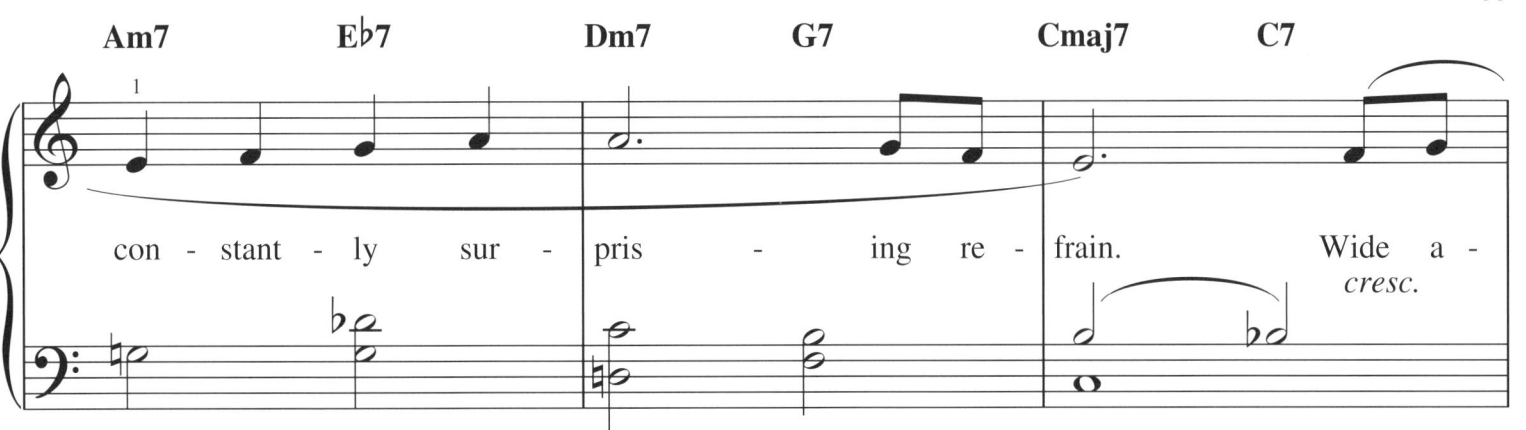
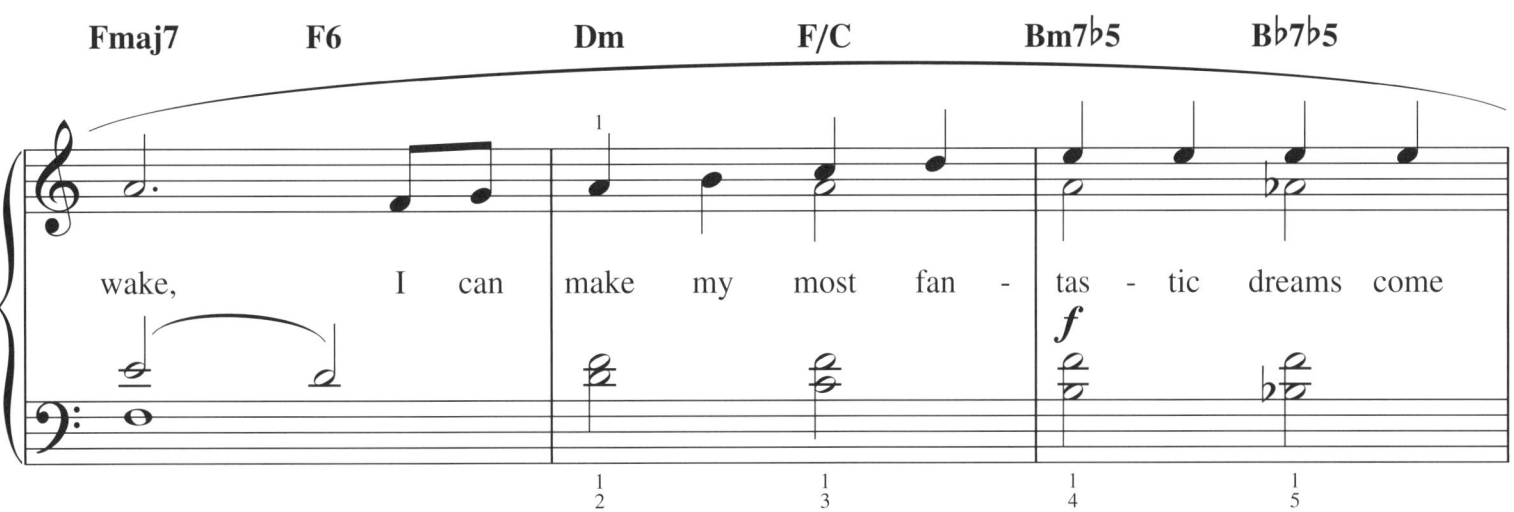
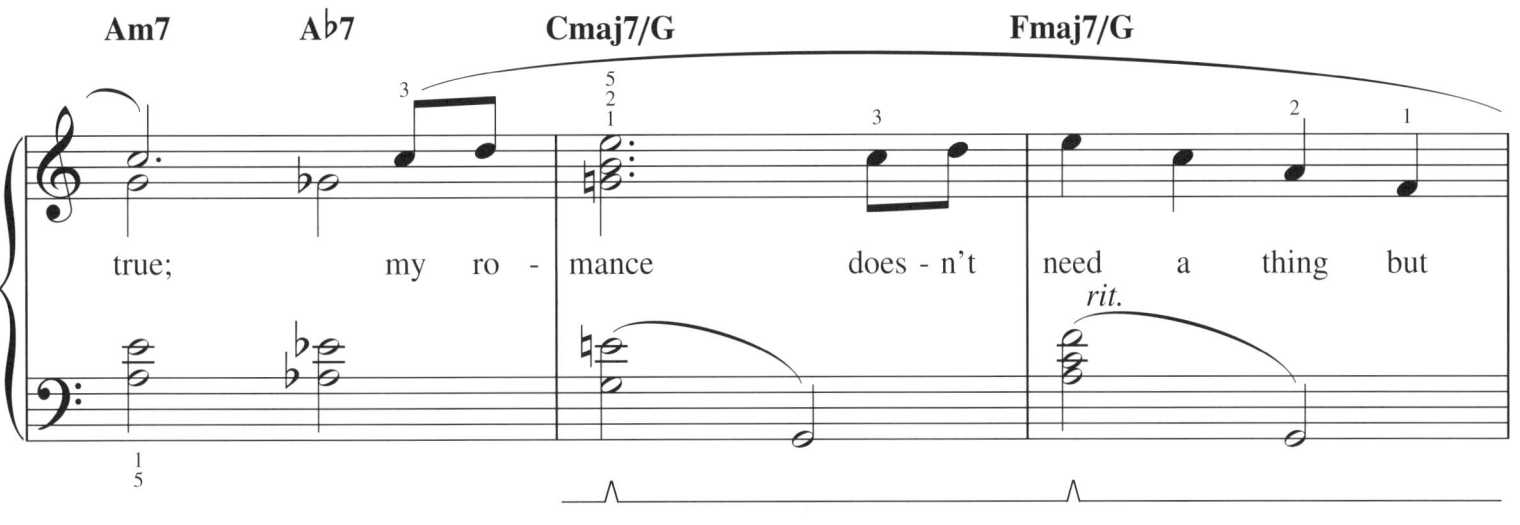
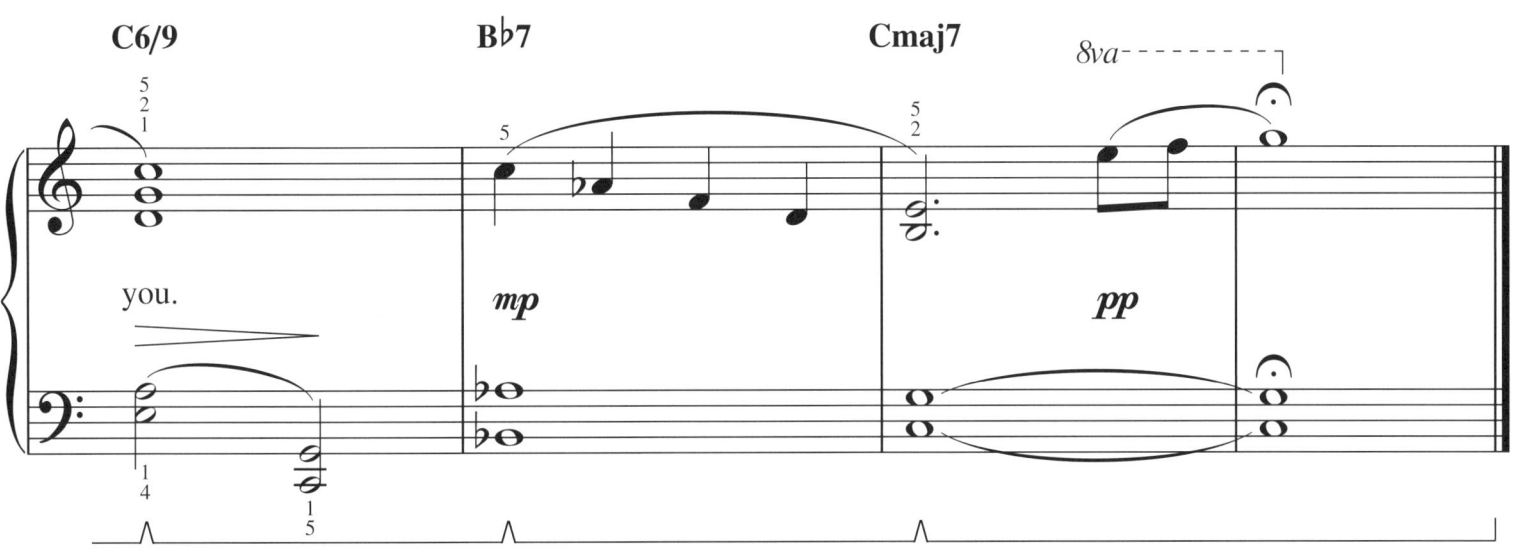

SAY IT ISN'T SO

Words and Music by IRVING BERLIN
Arranged by Phillip Keveren

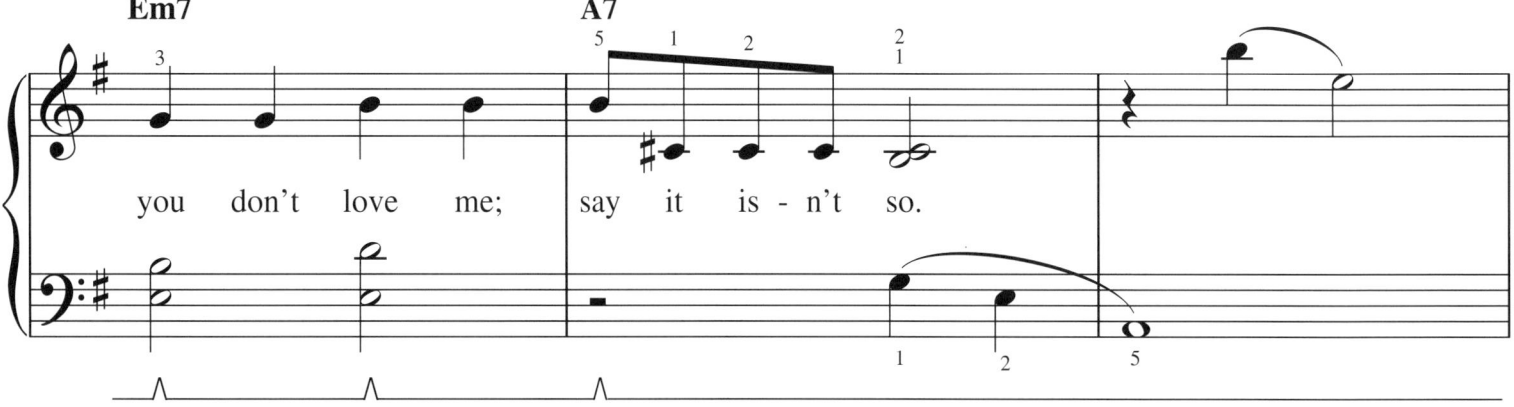

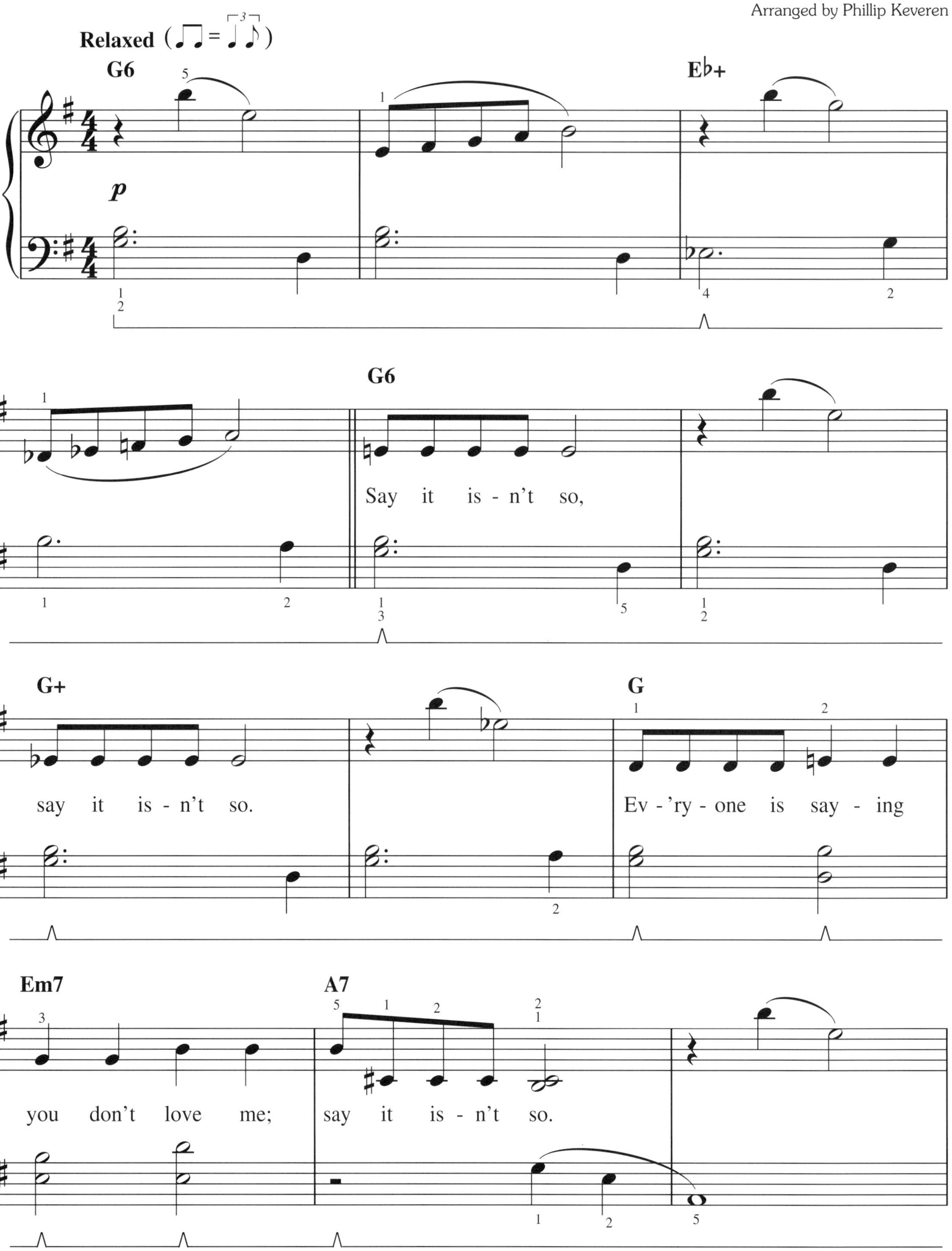

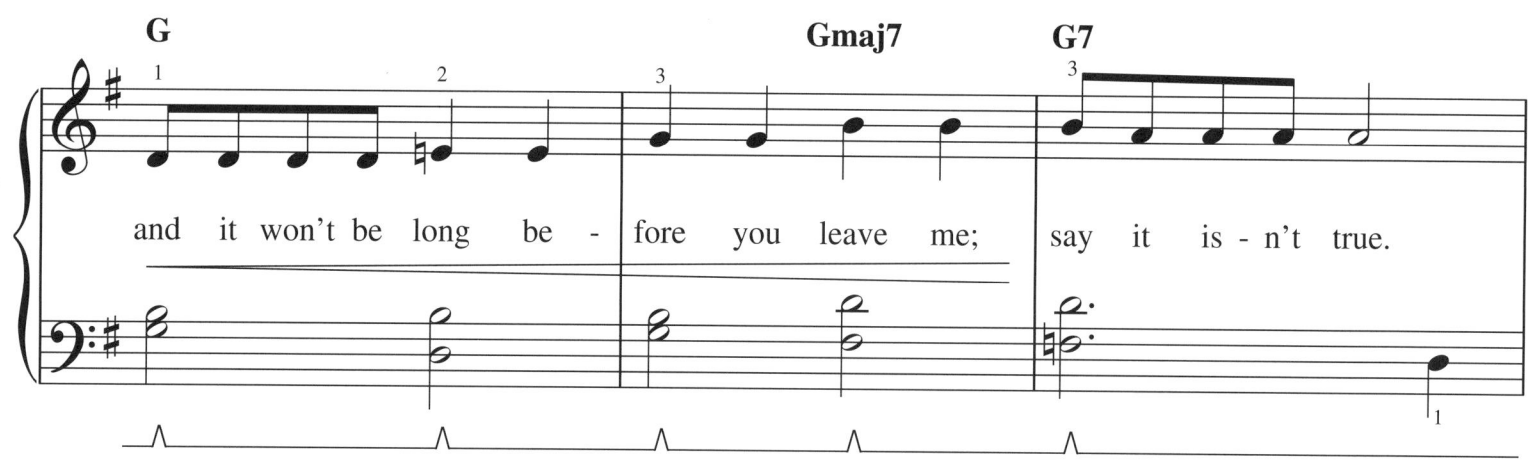
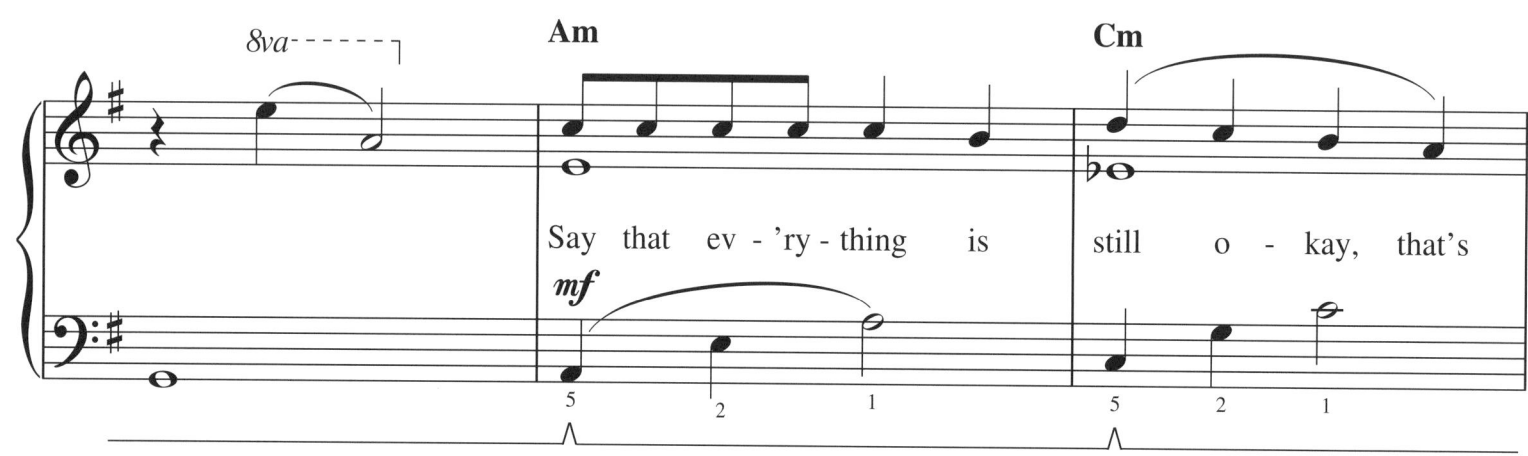
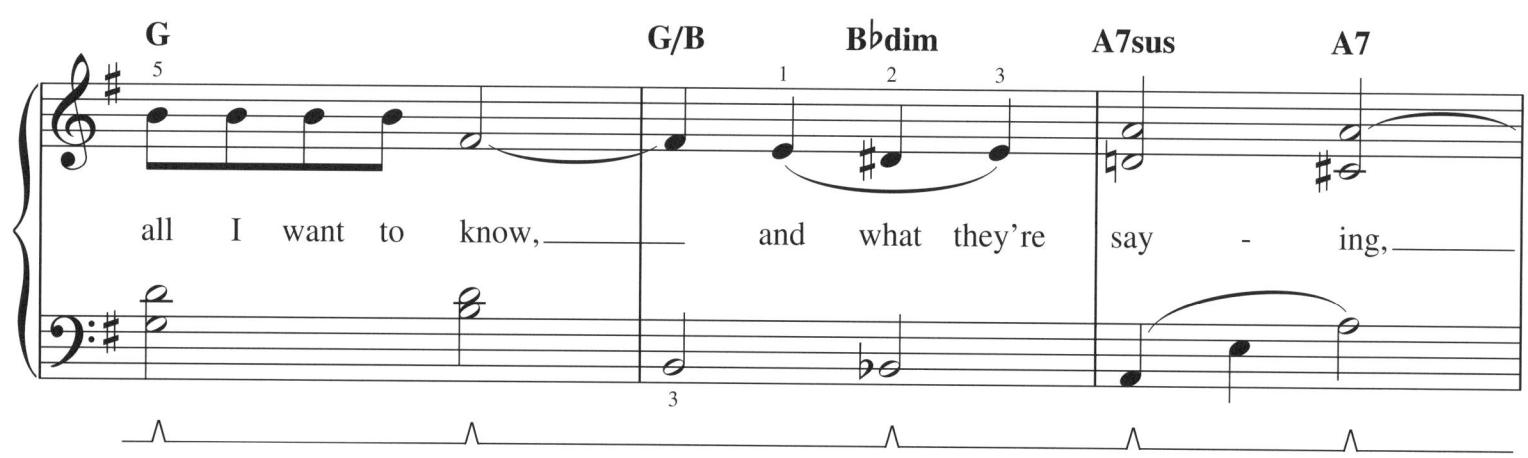
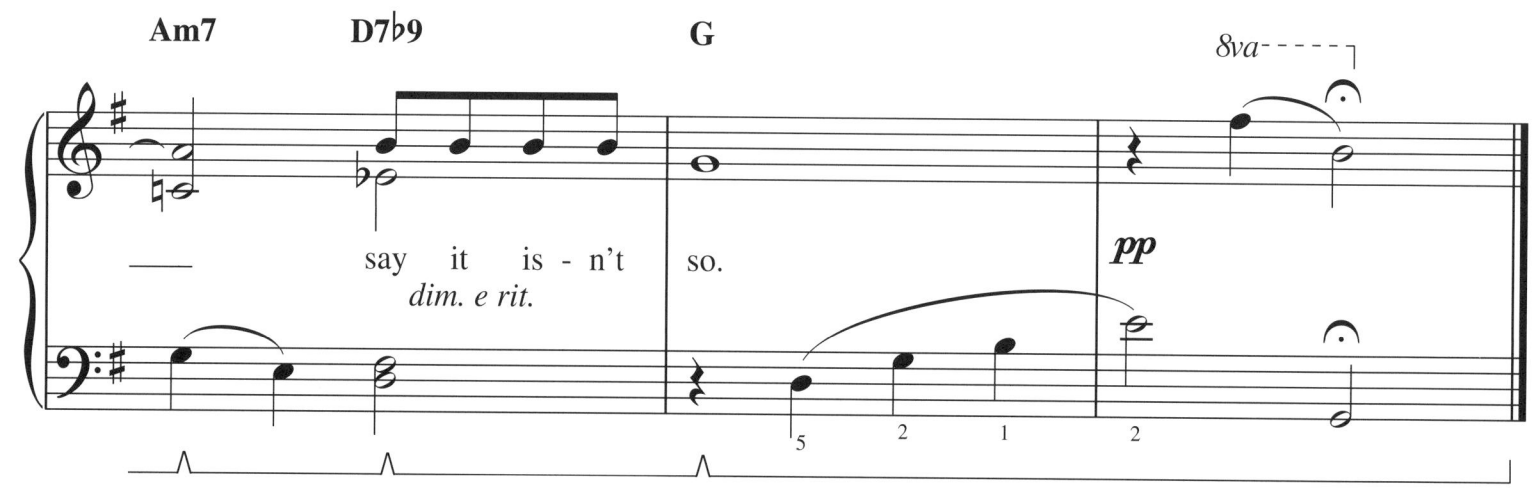

SKYLARK

Words by JOHNNY MERCER
Music by HOAGY CARMICHAEL
Arranged by Phillip Keveren

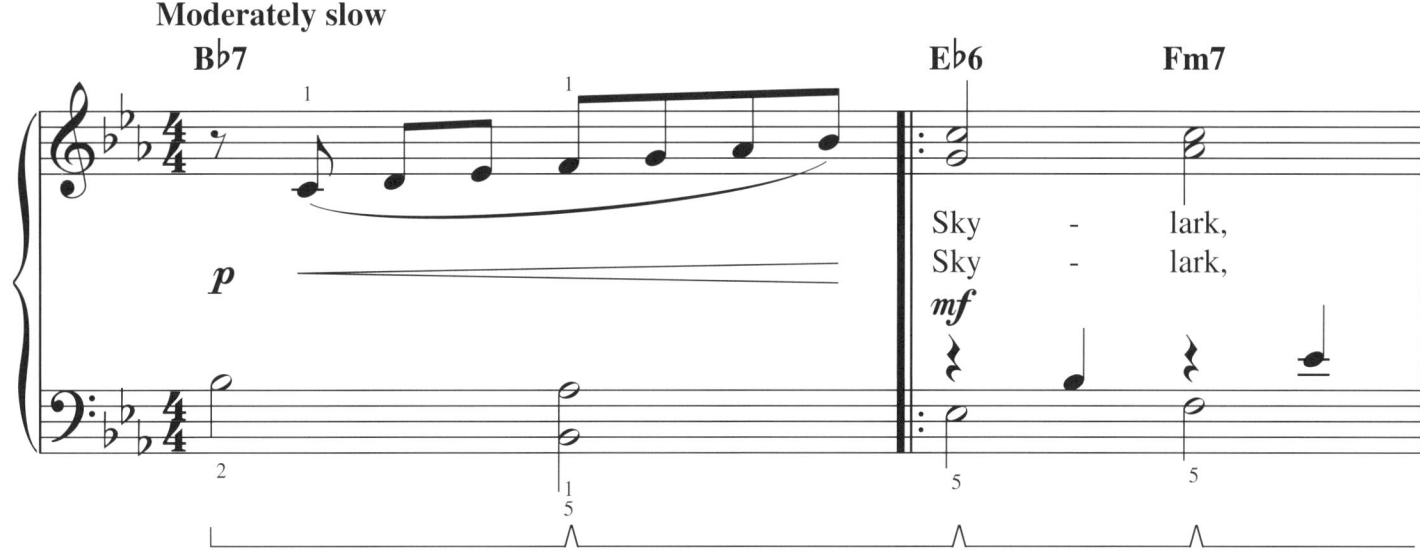
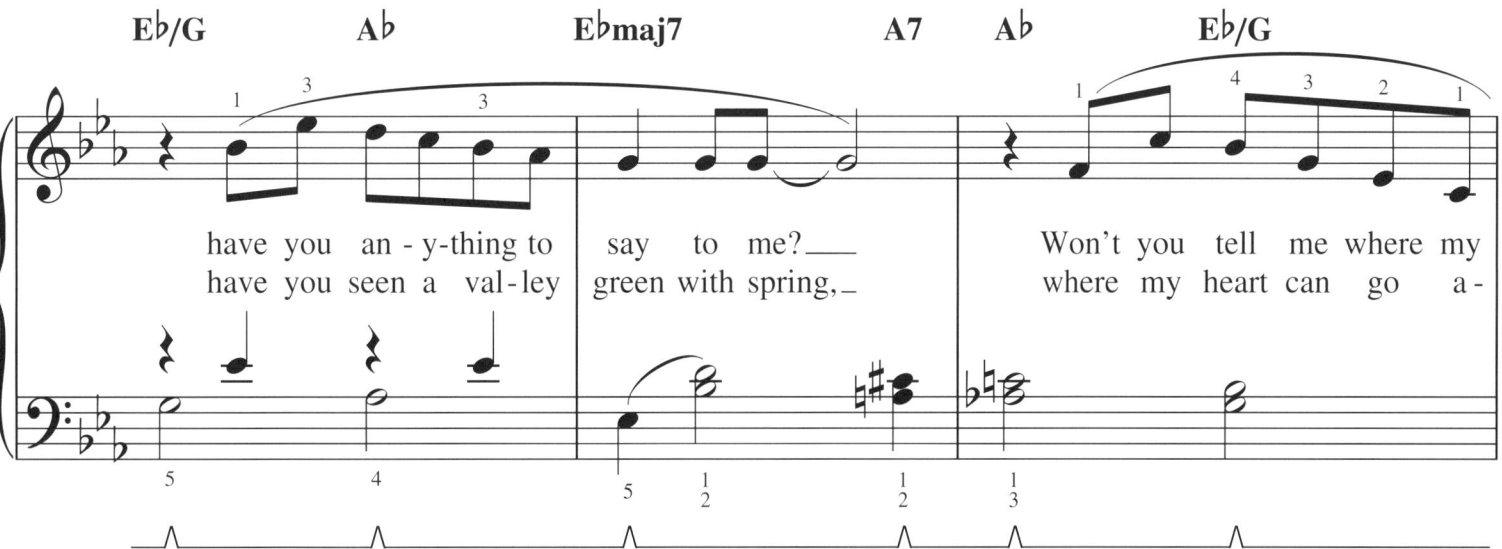
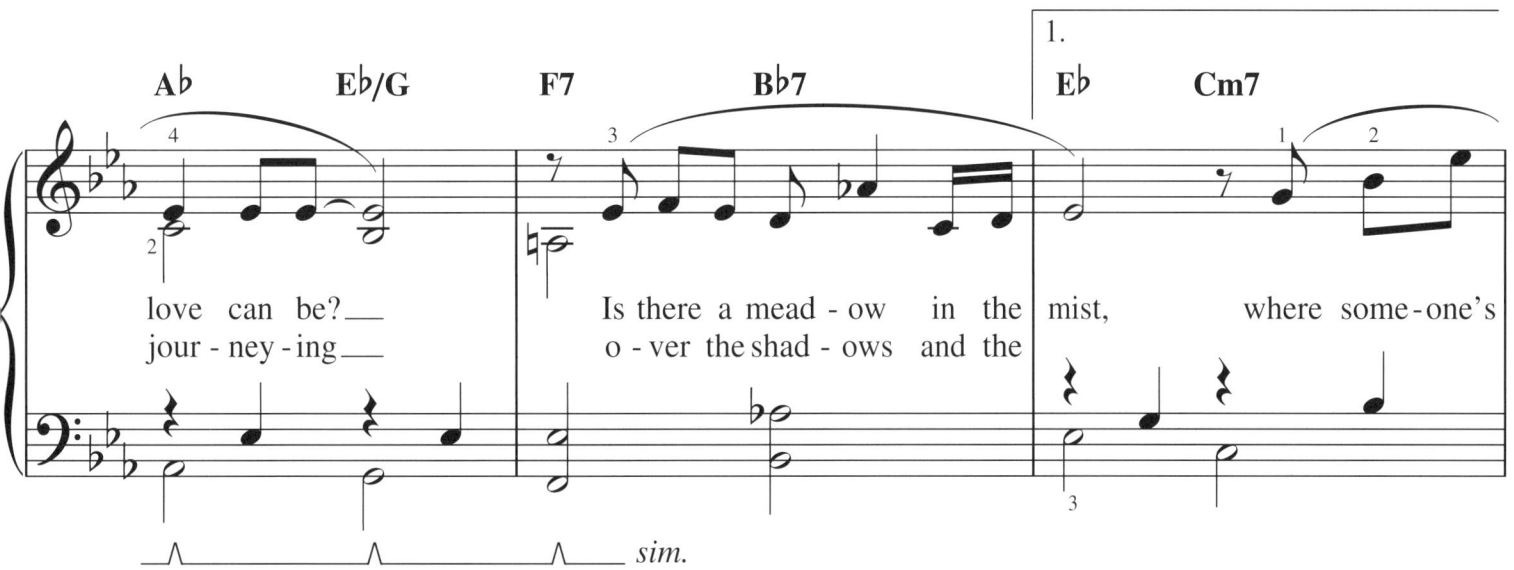

Copyright © 1941, 1942 by Songs Of Peer, Ltd. and WB Music Corp.
Copyright Renewed
International Copyright Secured   All Rights Reserved

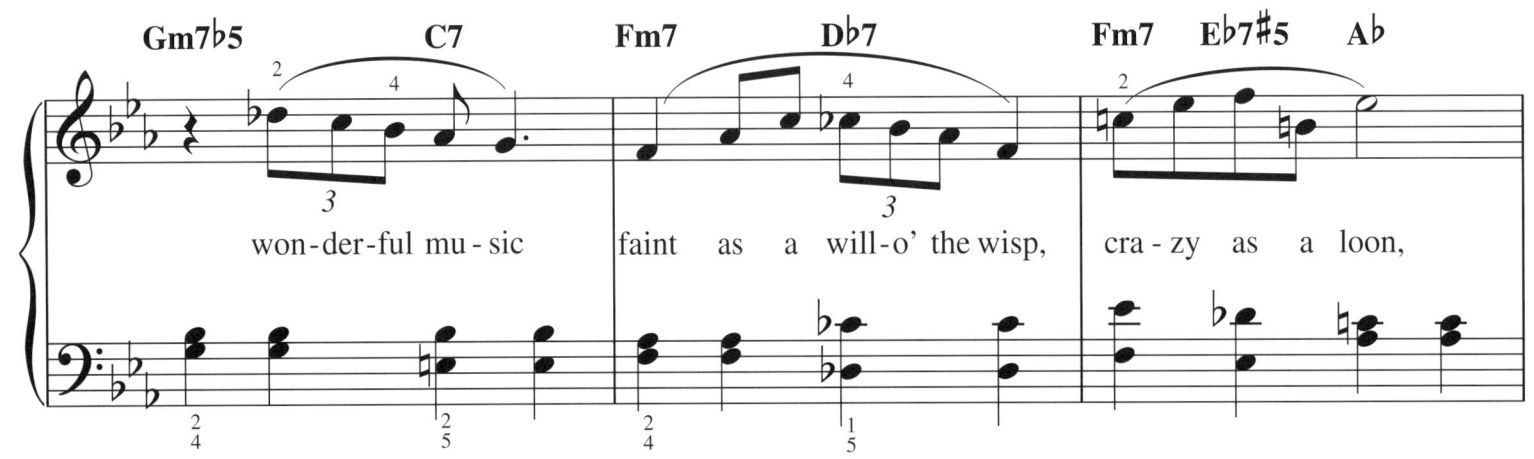

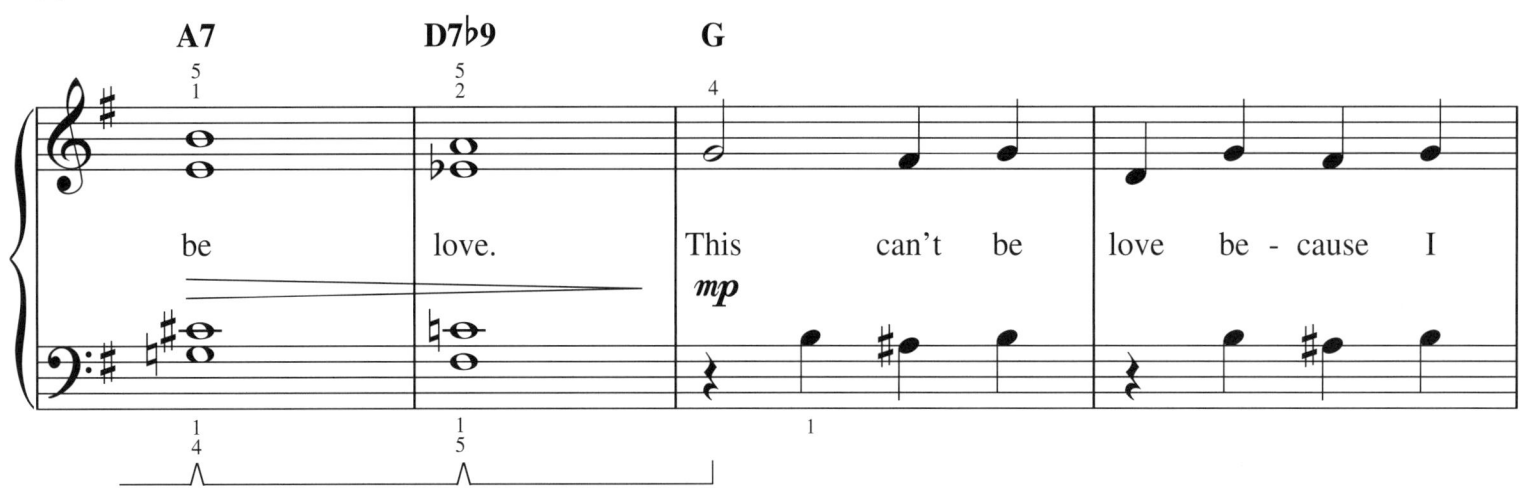
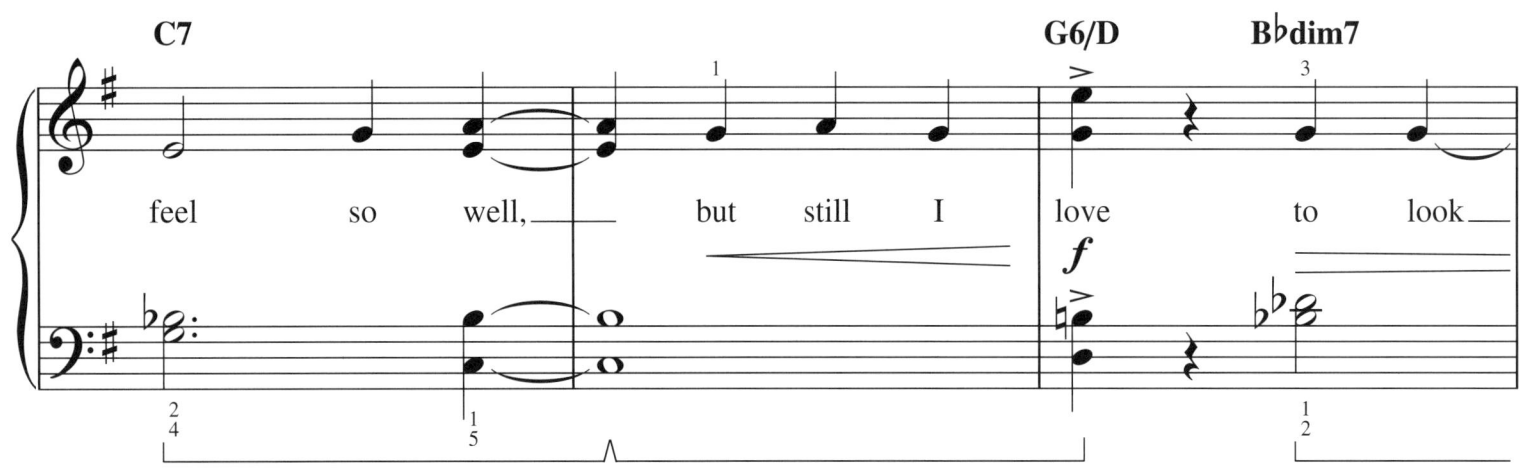
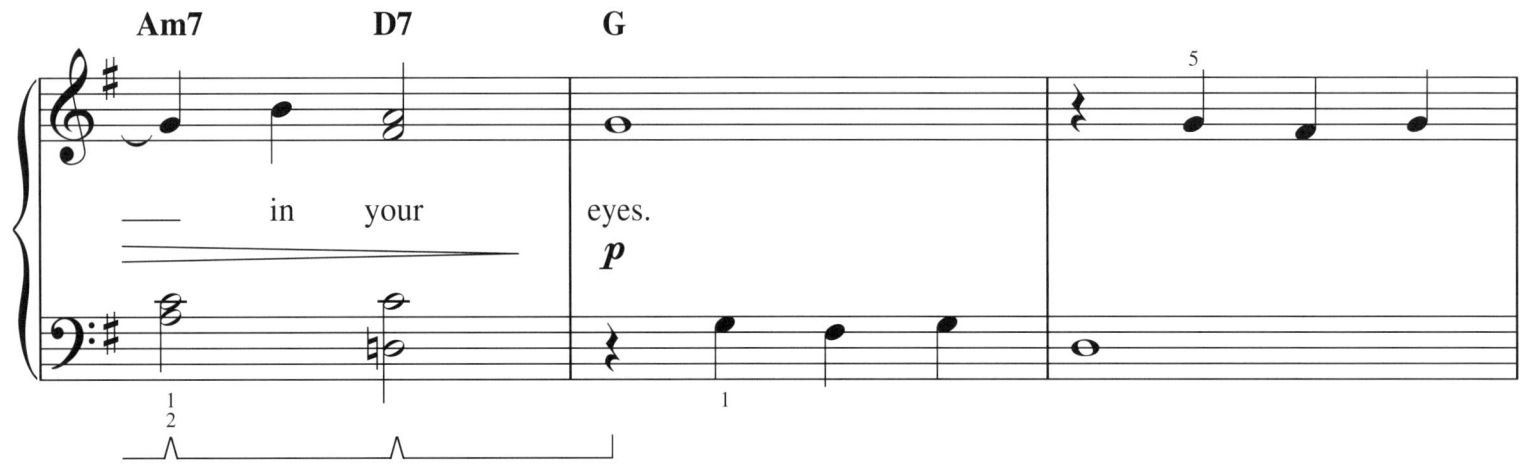
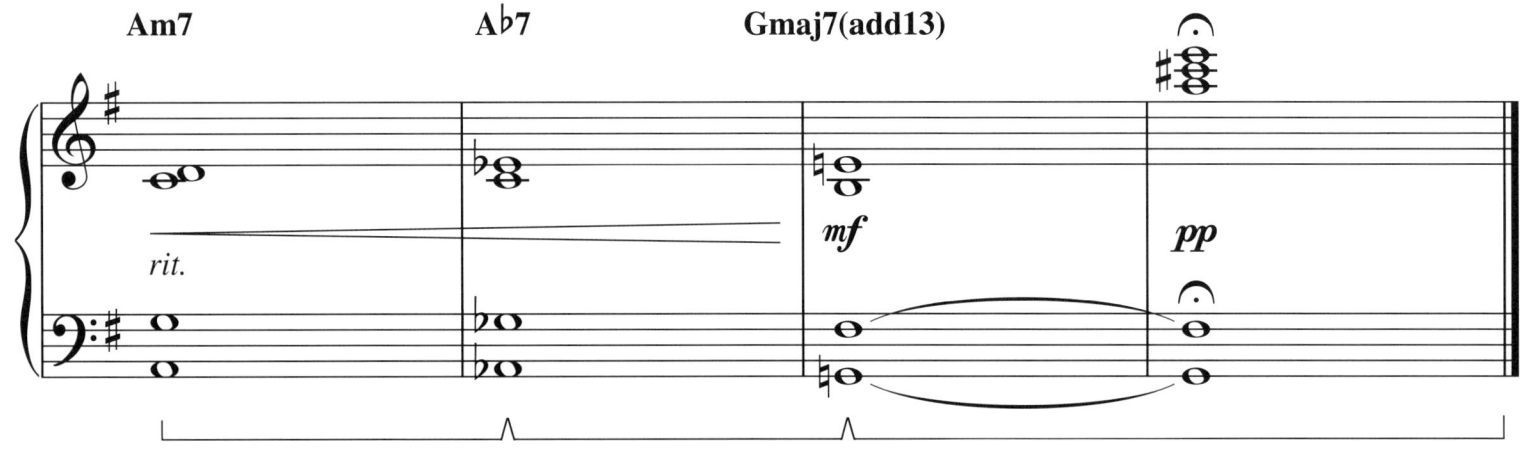

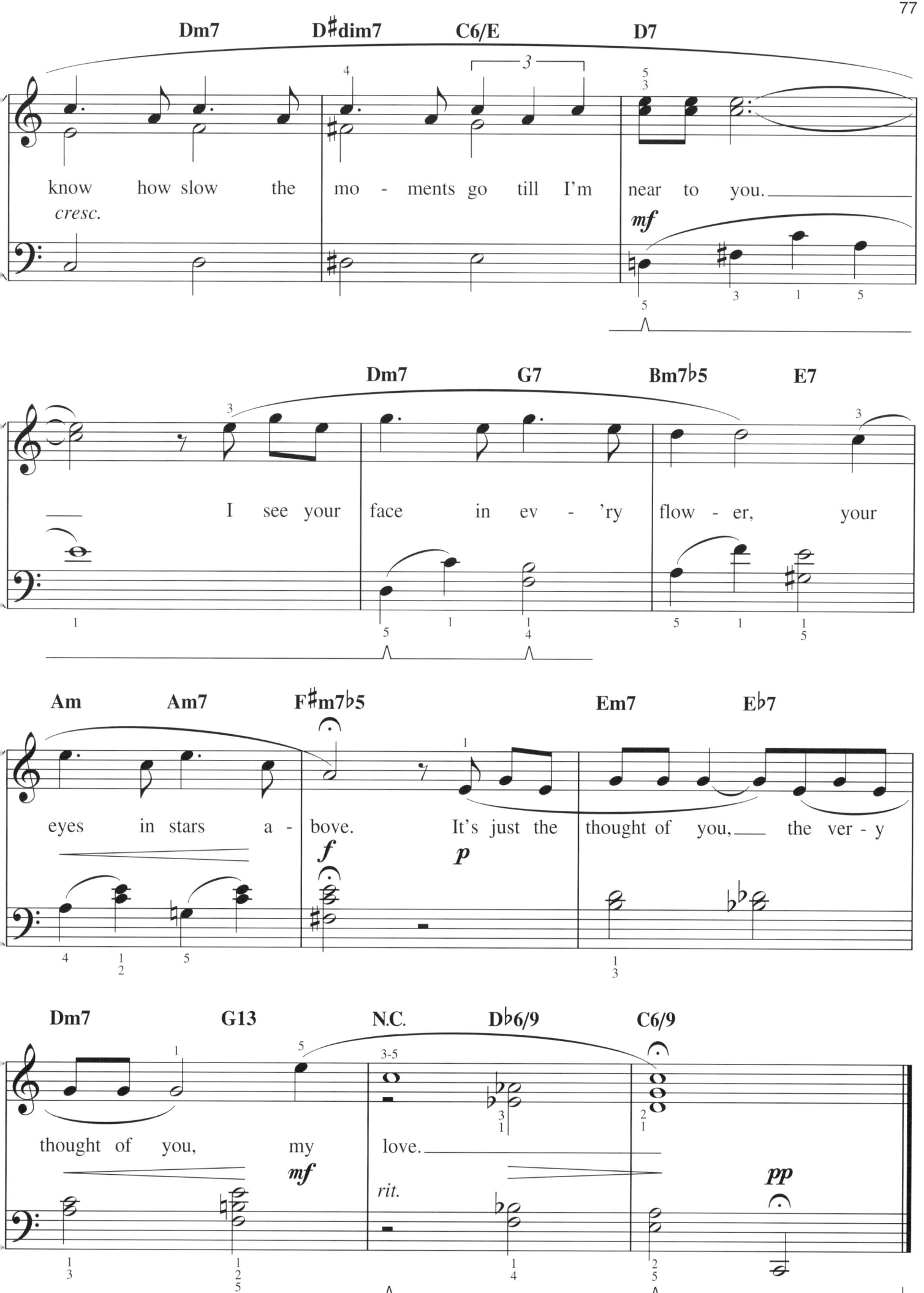

THE PHILLIP KEVEREN SERIES

PIANO SOLO —
Late Intermediate/Early Advanced Level

ABOVE ALL
00311024 ....$11.95

THE BEATLES
00306412 ....$12.95

BROADWAY'S BEST
00310669 ....$12.95

A CELTIC CHRISTMAS
00310629 ....$10.95

THE CELTIC COLLECTION
00310549 ....$12.95

CINEMA CLASSICS
00310607 ....$12.95

CLASSIC WEDDING SONGS
00311101 ....$10.95

CLASSICAL JAZZ
00311083 ....$12.95

CONTEMPORARY WEDDING SONGS
00311103 ....$12.95

GREAT STANDARDS
00311157 ....$12.95

THE HYMN COLLECTION
00311071 ....$10.95

HYMNS WITH A TOUCH OF JAZZ
00311249 ....$10.95

I COULD SING OF YOUR LOVE FOREVER
00310905 ....$12.95

JINGLE JAZZ
00310762 ....$12.95

LET FREEDOM RING!
00310839 ....$9.95

ANDREW LLOYD WEBBER
00313227 ....$14.95

RICHARD RODGERS – CLASSICS
00310755 ....$12.95

SHOUT TO THE LORD!
00310699 ....$12.95

SMOOTH JAZZ
00311158 ....$12.95

EASY PIANO —
Early Intermediate/Intermediate Level

AFRICAN-AMERICAN SPIRITUALS
00310610 ....$9.95

CELTIC DREAMS
00310973 ....$10.95

CHRISTMAS POPS
00311126 ....$12.95

A CLASSICAL CHRISTMAS
00310769 ....$10.95

CLASSICAL MOVIE THEMES
00310975 ....$10.95

EARLY ROCK 'N' ROLL
00311093 ....$10.95

GOSPEL TREASURES
00310805 ....$11.95

IMMORTAL HYMNS
00310798 ....$10.95

LOVE SONGS
00310744 ....$10.95

POP BALLADS
00220036 ....$12.95

SWEET LAND OF LIBERTY
00310840 ....$9.95

TIMELESS PRAISE
00310712 ....$12.95

TV THEMES
00311086 ....$10.95

21 GREAT CLASSICS
00310717 ....$11.95

BIG-NOTE PIANO —
Late Elementary/Early Intermediate Level

BELOVED HYMNS
00311067 ....$12.95

CHILDREN'S FAVORITE MOVIE SONGS
00310838 ....$10.95

CHRISTMAS MUSIC
00311247 ....$10.95

CONTEMPORARY HITS
00310907 ....$12.95

JOY TO THE WORLD
00310888 ....$10.95

THE NUTCRACKER
00310908 ....$8.95

THIS IS YOUR TIME
00310956 ....$10.95

BEGINNING PIANO SOLOS —
Elementary/Late Elementary Level

AWESOME GOD
00311202 ....$10.95

CHRISTIAN CHILDREN'S FAVORITES
00310837 ....$10.95

CHRISTMAS FAVORITES
00311246 ....$10.95

CHRISTMAS TRADITIONS
00311117 ....$9.95

EASY HYMNS
00311250 ....$10.95

KIDS' FAVORITES
00310822 ....$10.95

MOVIE MUSIC
00311213 ....$10.95

PIANO DUET —
Late Intermediate Level

PRAISE & WORSHIP DUETS
00311203 ....$11.95

For More Information, See Your Local Music Dealer,
Or Write To:

HAL•LEONARD® CORPORATION
7777 W. BLUEMOUND RD. P.O. BOX 13819 MILWAUKEE, WI 53213

Visit Hal Leonard online at www.halleonard.com

Prices, contents and availability subject to change without notice.

0606